COFFEE
ISN'T ROCKET SCIENCE

SÉBASTIEN RACINEUX • CHUNG-LENG TRAN
ILLUSTRATIONS BY YANNIS VAROUTSIKOS

COFFEE ISN'T ROCKET SCIENCE

A QUICK AND EASY GUIDE TO BUYING,
BREWING, SERVING, ROASTING, AND TASTING COFFEE

SÉBASTIEN RACINEUX • CHUNG-LENG TRAN
ILLUSTRATED BY YANNIS VAROUTSIKOS

TRANSLATION BY JACKIE SMITH,
IN ASSOCIATION WITH CAMBRIDGE PUBLISHING MANAGEMENT

BLACK DOG
& LEVENTHAL
PUBLISHERS
NEW YORK

CONTENTS

Chapter 1: Coffee miscellanea

Chapter 2: Making a coffee

Chapter 3: Roasting

Chapter 4: Cultivation

Chapter 5: Appendices

🫘🫘 : denotes EXPERT pages

CHAPTER

1

COFFEE MISCELLANEA

WHAT KIND OF COFFEE DRINKER ARE YOU?

Your first-ever cup as a teenager may have made you cringe, but chances are, you have now come around to liking coffee. It is a regular part of your day. But how exactly would you describe your relationship with coffee?

How many cups of coffee do you drink each day?

0	Better to measure it on a weekly basis
1–2	Moderation in all things
2–3	That's about my limit
3–4	Occasionally . . . well, okay, often
>5	Yes, I know; I'm trying to cut down

When do you drink your first coffee of the day?

- [ ] When I wake up, before I shower
- [ ] After my shower
- [ ] With breakfast
- [ ] When I get to the office
- [ ] After lunch

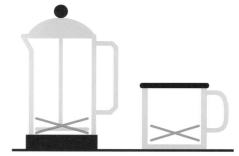

The coffee's run out!

- [ ] You find the nearest café and rush to the counter to order an espresso
- [ ] You head to the store, even if it's on the far side of town, to stock up on your favorite brand
- [ ] You go without, but you're cranky
- [ ] Oh well, you'll have a tea instead; that'll do the trick

You see yourself as:

☐ A coffee addict: You won't get anything out of me until I've had my fix.

☐ A coffee snob: Once you have learned to appreciate the finest coffees, you can never really go back.

☐ A romantic for whom the morning mug of coffee, croissant, and newspaper are sacrosanct. On the terrace in the sun is even better.

☐ A social drinker, with colleagues around the coffee machine.

☐ A takeout regular.

☐ Someone for whom "getting a cup of coffee" is a way of life.

☐ An occasional coffee drinker: I only really like it because it gives me an excuse to eat dessert.

☐ A wary coffee drinker: You allow yourself a decaf in the late evening.

COFFEES FOR EVERY TASTE

*We talk about having a cup of coffee,
but coffee comes in myriad sizes and guises!
You're sure to find one that suits you.*

ESPRESSO

A SMALL SERVING WITH A BIG FLAVOR, FOR THOSE WHO LOVE THE TASTE OF COFFEE.

DOUBLE ESPRESSO

FOR HARD WORKERS WHO KNOW THAT ONE SHOT IS JUST NOT ENOUGH.

MOCHA

FOR THOSE WHO AREN'T ACTUALLY THAT KEEN ON THE TASTE OF COFFEE BUT NEED A PICK-ME-UP. A COOL, CREATIVE SOLUTION.

LATTE

PERFECT FOR THE INDECISIVE: IT'S THE RISK-FREE MENU CHOICE.

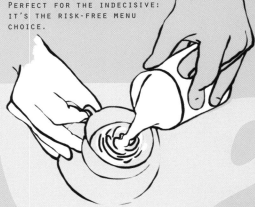

CAPPUCCINO

An easy-to-drink coffee for pleasure-seekers, but beware the milk moustache.

MACCHIATO

An easy-to-drink coffee for anyone who hates a milk moustache.

ICED COFFEE

A bold drink for those who like coffee as much as they like drinking through straws.

AMERICANO

One of the simple pleasures in life.

FRAPPUCCINO

A coffee treat for anyone who likes coffee almost as much as they like ice cream.

COFFEE AROUND THE WORLD

Coffee drinking habits vary according to people's tastes. But they also differ by region. Here's a quick roundup of coffee customs around the world.

IN THE UNITED STATES (AND OTHER ENGLISH-SPEAKING COUNTRIES) A

Most Americans drink coffee with milk, and usually have their drink to go. In diners and old-style coffee shops you can get a "bottomless cup of coffee." For the price of one coffee, the waitress will keep your mug topped up. This coffee tends to be very poor quality. It's brewed from low-grade beans and the coffeepot is kept constantly on the heat, sometimes all day. This is one of the main reasons for America's poor reputation for coffee.

IN ITALY B

Italy is the land of the espresso, where it is drunk strong and fast, standing at the counter. At about 11 a.m., which is *colazione* time (a short midmorning break halfway between breakfast and lunch), people commonly treat themselves to an espresso accompanied by a little pastry. At home, Italian *caffè moka* reigns supreme. The Italians do not drink filter coffee.

C

IN SCANDINAVIA (NORWAY, SWEDEN, ETC.)

The Scandinavians are the world's biggest consumers of coffee, which is drunk predominantly in the form of filter coffee. In nineteenth-century Norway it was common for people to produce their own spirits at home. Before long, to combat alcohol consumption, the Church decided to promote a less dangerous drink: coffee. And when home distillation was banned, coffee consumption became the norm, and has remained so ever since.

D

IN TURKEY

The technique used to make Turkish coffee (known as "Greek coffee" in Greece) can be traced back to the sixteenth century and the Ottoman Empire. It involves simmering coffee ground as fine as flour with water in a cezve, a traditional long-handled copper or brass pot. In the past, when it was served, the coffee used to be decanted into a coffeepot, called an ibrik, leaving the grounds behind. But now the terms cezve and ibrik have become synonymous, and coffee is served directly from the pot in which it is brewed. It can be served very sweet (*çok şekerli*), medium sweet (*az şekerli*), barely sweetened (*orta*), or without sugar (*sade*). After drinking, it used to be the custom to turn one's cup upside down in the saucer in order to read the future in the patterns left inside the cup by the coffee grounds. This coffee symbolizes a certain laid-back way of life, where time is spent chatting or hookah smoking. Incidentally, it is drunk not only in Turkey, but also in the Balkans and even the Middle East and northern Africa.

E

IN JAPAN

Japan is regarded first and foremost as tea country (producer and consumer), but the Japanese are also great coffee lovers and they have developed a real coffee culture since the eighteenth century. They also snap up many of the most expensive coffee lots in the world. They are great experts at the slow methods using the V60 or the vacuum (or "siphon") coffee maker, for example.

F

IN ETHIOPIA

It is traditionally the woman of the household who takes care of preparing coffee. First she roasts the green coffee beans in a pan. She then grinds the beans with a mortar and pestle and places the ground coffee in an earthenware coffeepot called a jebena. The coffee is poured into small, handleless cups, and popcorn is served to accompany it. This is known as the coffee ceremony.

WHERE TO GET A COFFEE

The diner, the deli, or fast-food restaurants used to be the place to go.
Then came Starbucks, and now smaller boutique chains and independent coffee shops
are springing up all over the place.

The coffee shop

It's the destination par excellence, particularly in urban locations in the United States. The clientele, typically young and online, see it as a "third place," somewhere between home and work. Your beverage is served by a barista, a specialist in coffee brewing. You can sit and drink it there, with a cookie or piece of cake, or take it out. You can also buy coffee beans there to use at home.

7 A.M.—8 P.M.

The café

An almost entirely European concept, this is where you go for the revered *petit noir* or "small black" consumed at the counter, but it doesn't only serve coffee. In France, for example, bistros or cafés are often the heart and soul of a village, district, or street. You can get a glass of wine, a beer or a soft drink, or have a cup of coffee, and some even serve lunch, tea, or dinner. The waiters serve the *petit noir* at the counter or bring it to your table, either indoors or outdoors. The price of your coffee varies according to where you decide to consume it.

7 A.M.–11 P.M.

THE COFFEE FAMILY

A botanical perspective on coffee beans.

Coffee plants

Ninety-nine percent of the world's coffee production comes from two species of coffee plant: *Coffea arabica*, or arabica, as it's commonly known, which comes from the word "Arab") and *Coffea canephora* (or robusta). They both belong to the genus *Coffea* (which encompasses around seventy species of coffee plant), which in turn belongs to the wider family of *Rubiaceae*. *Coffea liberica* and *Coffea excelsa* are also cultivated in West Africa and in Asia (largely for local consumption), but account for less than 2 percent of global output.

FAMILY	GENUS	SPECIES	VARIETIES
RUBIACEAE ·········	COFFEA ·········	┌··· ARABICA ··········	┌··· TYPICA
			└··· BOURBON
		└··· CANEPHORA ············	ROBUSTA

Arabica *vs* Robusta

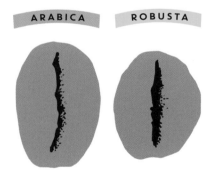

ARABICA   ROBUSTA

	COFFEA ARABICA	COFFEA CANEPHORA
NUMBER OF CHROMOSOMES	44	22
ALTITUDE	2,000–8,000 FT	0–2,300 FT
TEMPERATURE	59–75°F	75–86°F
POLLINATION	SELF-POLLINATION	CROSS-POLLINATION
FLOWERING	AFTER RAIN	IRREGULAR
MATURITY	6–9 MONTHS	10–11 MONTHS
CAFFEINE CONTENT	0.6–1.4%	1.8–4%

ROBUSTA? IT'S NOT THAT GREAT...

Robusta is the main variety of *C. canephora* to be produced and marketed. Its flavor qualities are poor; its only benefit is that it is cheaper and easier to produce. It also contains more caffeine. It is used primarily for instant coffee, in espresso blends in Italy and Portugal, and in vending machines.

VARIETIES, HYBRIDS, AND MUTATIONS

You can find details of the different species and varieties on pages 132 and 133.

THE COFFEE TRADE

Coffee, as a commodity, is traded globally in various ways.

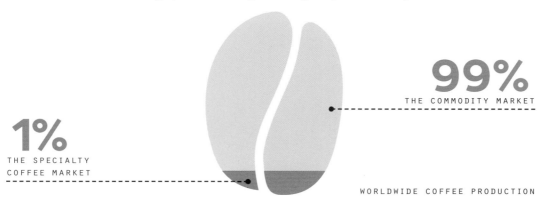

99%
THE COMMODITY MARKET

1%
THE SPECIALTY
COFFEE MARKET

WORLDWIDE COFFEE PRODUCTION

The "specialty" coffee market

Specialty coffees account for approximately 1 percent of global output. These are coffees rated at least 80/100, whose price is determined not by the commodity market, but by their quality and rarity. This is part of a new general market approach that is now emerging, whereby the producer cultivates different botanical varieties depending on the nature of the terroir, the roaster devises roasting profiles for each kind of coffee bean, and the barista is always on a quest to improve the way the coffee is brewed. It may be a niche market, but it has wrought changes in the way coffee is produced and consumed; coffee, a basic necessity, consumed for its stimulating effects, has become a precious and complex product in the same way that wine is. Coffee is no longer simply drunk; it is savored.

The commodity market

This is the market on which commodities are bought and sold. Coffee is traded on the New York exchanges in the case of Arabica and in London in the case of Robusta. The price, which is very variable, fluctuating according to supply and demand as well as the speculative behavior of the various market players (traders, pension funds, etc.), is expressed in dollars per pound (454 g) of coffee. Neither the quality of the coffee nor the costs of production are taken into account, something that presents a problem for coffee producers who find themselves no longer able to make a living from their work. To combat this trend, various initiatives have been put in place, including "fair trade," which ensures that coffee farmers are able to earn a decent income.

Fair trade

Fair trade certification

Fair trade certification was set up in the Netherlands in 1988 by the Max Havelaar Foundation with the aim of guaranteeing a purchase price deemed fair for small coffee producers. If prices trend down, the fair trade label guarantees producers a minimum amount that they can live on. If prices rise above the benchmark, the price will then be increased by a predetermined value.

Fair trade principles
Fair trade is based on three principles:
• a sustainable minimum price (but no minimum quantity);
• environmental conservation (encouraging organic production, no GMOs);
• a social component (collective equipment financing).

Limits of the fair trade mark
• It is not possible for a single farm to obtain this certification; it has to be part of a cooperative.
• When fair trade products started to be sold in large supermarkets, the certification label was forced to work with large farms in order to meet demand, whereas fair trade was created for small producers.
• This certification does not amount to a quality label as such.

THE COFFEE PROFESSIONALS

A lot of work happens before you take the first sip of your morning coffee!
The journey from bean to cup involves a whole series of steps and processes.

The producer

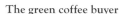

Coffee plantations are tended by a coffee farmer. The coffee farmer, or producer, is someone who lives close to the land. At harvest time, he gathers the coffee cherries, then dries them by one of various processes to extract the beans from them.

The green coffee buyer

The coffee buyer travels around coffee-producing countries to select green coffee beans and negotiate a deal, then sells them on to the coffee roaster, or merchant. He takes care of the logistics of transporting the bags to the consumer countries where the beans will be roasted.

The roaster

To unlock all their flavors, the green coffee beans have to be heated and tumbled simultaneously. At the roasting house, this is the job of the roaster, who adjusts the roasting process according to the type of bean in order to produce the best possible results. These days the role of the roaster is changing, with more and more roasters traveling to the producer countries themselves to select their own coffee beans.

The barista

The barista, the final link in the coffee chain, is more than merely a waiter. A great connoisseur of coffee, he serves the concoction that he has expertly prepared, transforming the roasted beans into a drink on demand. He also advises customers on the different coffee varieties, flavors, and methods of preparation (espresso, slow methods, etc.), and sells coffee beans.

COFFEE LINGO

If you want to understand the world of coffee, there are some words you need to know!

Grand cru is the name given to a coffee bean variety noted for its flavor qualities. You just need to know how to get it to release its full potential!

Grind size is a measure of how finely the coffee is ground.

Latte art is the name of the technique in which a design is drawn in the milk foam of a cappuccino.

A **batch** is the quantity of coffee roasted at one time.

A **barista** is the coffee expert who crafts the drink you actually get to consume. The coffee shop is where you'll find him!

A **blend** is a mix of coffees of different origin (different regions, countries etc.)

Coffee makers are the appliances commonly used for making coffee, from the mildest brew to the strongest.

The **cherry** is the name of the fruit of the coffee plant. It contains one or two coffee beans.

Roasting is the process of cooking the coffee beans. The word **roaster** designates both the roasting expert and the machine used to perform this process.

MILD

CHEMEX

SIPHON

V60

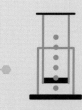

AEROPRESS

The **basket** is another name for the filter on an espresso machine.

A **shot** is a single 1-ounce portion of espresso. It is drunk in one go.

The **kettle** is a familiar kitchen appliance. But in the world of coffee, "kettle" refers to the typical coffee kettle with its gooseneck spout, which is a must-have when preparing filter coffees.

Filter coffees, gentle methods, slow methods: These are synonymous terms referring to coffees not prepared by a fast method under high pressure, like espresso.

A **tamper** is the special tool the barista uses to pack or "tamp" down the ground coffee in the filter.

Calibrating an espresso means adjusting the various parameters involved in making an espresso.

A coffee is said to be **clean** in reference to its clarity.

Cupping is a standard tasting method for judging the quality of the coffee.

During roasting, the bean produces a characteristic noise, rather like popcorn: the **crack**.

The **burrs** are the part of the coffee grinder that grinds the beans.

Ground coffee is referred to as the **grounds**.

FRENCH PRESS

MOKA POT

ESPRESSO MACHINE

IBRIK

STRONG

THE TROUBLE WITH COFFEE...

There are many myths surrounding coffee. Are they true or false?
Here are some answers from a reliable source.

Coffee is a diuretic and a laxative!

Coffee increases secretion of stomach acid, which aids digestion.

It takes five minutes for caffeine to reach the brain. Caffeine has a half-life of three to five hours. This refers to the period of time after which its effects are halved.

Consume in moderation!
Is coffee a drug? No, not strictly speaking. But if someone who consumes a lot of coffee (more than 400 mg of caffeine a day) goes cold turkey, it will take three to five days for the symptoms—irritability, headaches and temporary tiredness—to disappear.

It seems that coffee helps to prevent certain diseases: It is thought to slow the progression of Parkinson's disease in men. Caffeine is also believed to improve memory function in Alzheimer's sufferers. The polyphenols (antioxidants) contained in coffee are believed to counteract type 2 diabetes. Some sixty studies have shown that coffee plays a part in preventing several types of cancer (bladder, mouth, colon, esophageal, uterine, brain, skin, liver, and breast).

Coffee is bad for your nerves!!
Caffeine has a stimulating effect that makes you more alert, increases your heart rate, enhances cognitive function, reduces fatigue, and improves your reaction times.

Although it is true that coffee can stain your teeth, caffeine and polyphenols (or phenolic compounds) have antibacterial properties that help to prevent tooth decay.

Excessive consumption (more than 400 mg/day of caffeine) of coffee as well as drinking coffee too close to bedtime can make it **hard to drop off to sleep** and can cause insomnia. Excessive caffeine intake can also cause palpitations and anxiety.

Caffeine improves physical performance, particularly endurance, by converting fat into energy. Caffeine was even included on the list of substances banned under the World Anti-Doping Code until 2004.

A filter coffee contains more caffeine than an espresso: a cup of espresso contains 47 to 75 mg; a mug of filter coffee, 75 to 200 mg.

What else?

2

MAKING A COFFEE

GRINDING YOUR COFFEE

Whatever your preferred brewing method—filter coffee or espresso—you will need to use ground coffee. Everyone knows that coffee powder is produced by grinding the roasted coffee beans in a coffee grinder. What people don't tend to realize, though, is that different models of grinder give a finer or coarser grind, producing ground coffee exhibiting different qualities and suitable for different uses. So it is important to consider your choice of grinder carefully if you want to be sure of obtaining your perfect shot.

Why invest in a grinder?

Given that coffee merchants are able to produce different grinds for different brewing methods, there seems to be little need to own your own coffee grinder. But whether you are a newcomer to the world of coffee or a well-informed enthusiast, here are two good reasons to invest in one. The fact is, you cannot really be a true espresso connoisseur if you don't own a coffee grinder. For a filter coffee drinker, it is less essential. Whatever the case, a coffee grinder will guarantee you an exceptional coffee!

GRIND SIZE: A MEASURE OF THE FINENESS OF THE GRIND

1

COFFEE THAT IS ALWAYS FRESH

Ground coffee does not keep well. The transformation of beans into powder produces two associated reactions: the release of CO_2, a natural preservative contained in the beans, and the acceleration of the oxidation of the aromatic essential oils in the coffee (known as caffeol or caffeone) and other flavor components when they come into contact with the ambient air. So once the packet is open, while coffee beans can keep for several days, for ground coffee the storage time is no more than a few hours.

2

CONTROLLING THE FINENESS OF THE GRIND

The fineness of the grind (or grind size) is a fundamental variable that can be adjusted according to the desired result and other parameters. The espresso extraction time and the coffee balance are affected by the temperature and humidity of the air. Hence the barista has to adjust the grind size several times a day. This is why it is not advisable to buy coffee that has already been ground to a certain fixed grind size.

The right grind for each brewing method

Different methods of brewing coffee require different grind sizes. Adjusting the grind size allows you to vary the speed of extraction of the coffee's flavor molecules. The finer the grind, the greater the surface area in contact with the solvent—in this case, water—and the faster the coffee components dissolve: espresso needs fine-ground coffee to compensate for the fact that the brewing time is short (less than 30 seconds), whereas a French press, with its four-minute infusing time, requires a coarse grind, which helps keep bitterness to a minimum and limits the amount of sediment in the cup.

WHAT GRIND FOR WHAT METHOD?

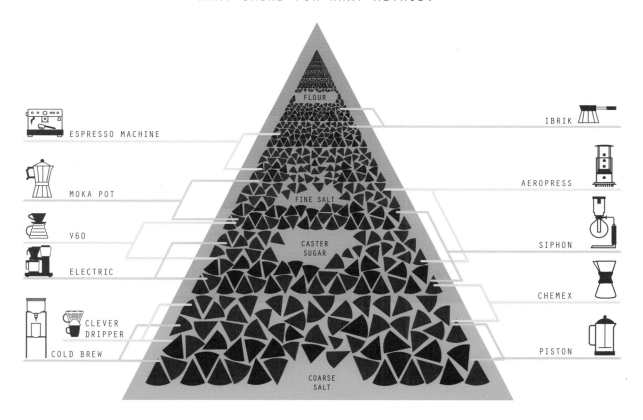

ESPRESSO MACHINE

MOKA POT

V60

ELECTRIC

CLEVER DRIPPER

COLD BREW

FLOUR

FINE SALT

CASTER SUGAR

COARSE SALT

IBRIK

AEROPRESS

SIPHON

CHEMEX

PISTON

WHY IS A SIZE RANGE STATED FOR EACH METHOD, RATHER THAN SIMPLY A SINGLE SPECIFIED SIZE?

Because there are other variables involved:
• the coffee bean itself (variety, density, roast level, etc.);
• the coffee dose required (the higher the dose weight, the coarser the grind required);
• the time elapsed since roasting (a fine grind can compensate for a lack of freshness);
• climate conditions (humid air calls for a coarser grind) . . .

COFFEE GRINDERS

From the manual coffee grinder to the latest model stacked with electronics, the mechanical principle is always the same: to break and grind the coffee beans by passing them between two burrs—one of them rotating, the other fixed. The fineness of the resulting powder, or grind, depends on the size of the gap between the two grinding wheels.

For decades a feature of every home, the manual grinder later seemed doomed to be relegated to junk shops and specialist collections. It has now reclaimed its place and is once again popular with coffee connoisseurs.

Originally sold by large chains of coffee shops, today these are available everywhere.

The grinder traditionally used in bars and restaurants for making espresso.

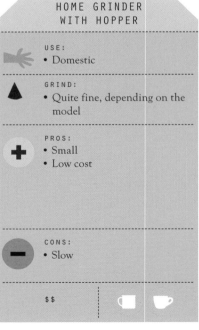

MANUAL GRINDER

USE:
• Domestic use or on the move

GRIND:
• Suitable for filter coffee

PROS:
• A nice object with an attractive design, whether it's a vintage or contemporary model, featuring wear-resistant ceramic burrs.
• Compact, transportable, inexpensive, doesn't need electricity

CONS:
• Elbow grease required!
• Not a very consistent grind

$

HOME GRINDER WITH HOPPER

USE:
• Domestic

GRIND:
• Quite fine, depending on the model

PROS:
• Small
• Low cost

CONS:
• Slow

$ $

ESPRESSO GRINDER WITH DOSER

USE:
• Professional or domestic

GRIND:
• Fine

PROS:
• Can grind very fine
• The doser churns the ground coffee and breaks up any clumps.

CONS:
• Grounds left in the doser deteriorate.

$ $ $

This grinder was designed for customers who like to buy their coffee ground on demand.

Invented by the German company Mahlkönig, the "doserless" grinder grinds on demand and delivers one or two programmed doses of ground coffee directly to the filter basket.

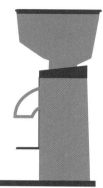

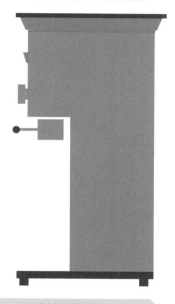

TWO KINDS OF GRIND REGULATOR

1. Regulator with stepped adjustment: the more steps there are, the more accurate you can be.

2. Regulator with continuous adjustment (stepless). This allows the grain size to be more precisely controlled. It is therefore a better option when preparing espresso.

DOSERLESS ESPRESSO GRINDER

 USE:
- Professional or domestic

 GRIND:
- Fine and always fresh

 PROS:
- The freshly ground coffee does not have time to go stale.
- Can grind very fine

 CONS:
- Produces clumps

$$$$

COMMERCIAL GRINDER

 USE:
- Professional

 GRIND:
- Not always uniform

 PROS:
- Its large capacity enables it to grind large quantities of coffee in a short time.

 CONS:
- Regulation of grind fineness not very accurate

$$$$$

WHAT ABOUT BLADED GRINDERS?

They work on the same principle as a meat and vegetable mini chopper: the longer you leave it running, the finer the output. They are not expensive and give a uniform grind. Useful if you want to achieve a balanced coffee …

TYPES OF BURRS

Coffee grinders fall into two categories—burr grinders and blade grinders.
A burr grinder comes with either flat or conical burrs.

Shapes available

Flat burrs
Flat burrs give a reasonably uniform grind and very little ground coffee is left behind in the grind chamber.

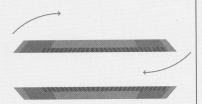

Conical burrs
A lot of entry-level domestic grinders come equipped with burrs of this kind. Paradoxically, on professional grinders, their low rotational speed means they need either a powerful motor or a system of gears, which makes the grinder more expensive to buy.

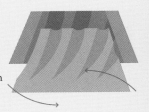

 This type of burr is best suited to grinders for home use or small-scale professional use (less than 7 lb/day) used at regular intervals throughout the day.

 Grinders with conical burrs are aimed more at large-scale commercial users (more than 7 lb/day). They are able to cope during peak periods as they perform best in continuous operation.

The A fresh and consistent grind.

The These burrs rotate more slowly (about 400 rpm), which prevents the grounds from heating up and gives the coffee a nice texture.

The They have to rotate at high speed (about 1,500 rpm) and, if used intensively, tend to warm the grounds, forming oily clumps and potentially causing the flavors to evaporate.

The With these burrs, a lot of ground coffee is left behind in the grind chamber. This may, if the grinder is inactive for a few minutes, impinge on the freshness of the delivered dose.

Durability

Over time, the burr edges become blunted. Signs of wear include a longer grind time, the presence of clumps indicating that the grounds are being heated, and a deterioration in the quality of the resulting coffee (less crema on the espresso, lackluster flavors …). As a general guide, you might expect a coffee shop to change its burrs once a year, and a private user once every twenty years.

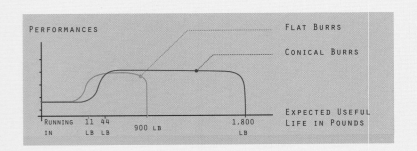

Materials

CERAMIC

HARD BUT BRITTLE, VULNERABLE TO FOREIGN BODIES, SUCH AS STONES THAT MAY SOMETIMES BE MIXED IN WITH THE COFFEE BEANS

STEEL & TITANIUM

OFFER THE BENEFIT OF BEING HARD-WEARING WITHOUT BREAKING

MAINTAINING YOUR GRINDER

Your grinder is inevitably going to get messy.
It is important to keep the parts clean so as not to spoil the purity of the brew.

 ① HOPPER

How? Sponge + liquid dish soap.
How often? As soon as you see oily marks and traces of silvery coating appear on the surfaces.

② BODY

How? A slightly soapy sponge + a microfiber cloth to remove any unsightly marks.
How often? Every day.

③ DOSER

Why? Grounds are retained in the interior of the doser.
How? A special brush to remove any particles stuck around the edges and in the gaps. For a more thorough clean, use the nozzle of a vacuum cleaner.
How often? Every day, or even several times a day.

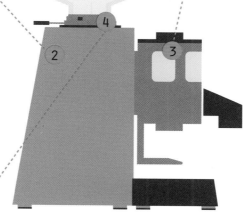

④ GRIND CHAMBER

Why? The grind chamber and the burrs collect grounds and coffee oils on all their internal surfaces, which then go stale.
How? Insert a vacuum cleaner nozzle into the exit chute and the grind chamber intake. Two ways of accessing the nooks and crannies:
• Remove the fixed upper burr to access the central part of the chamber. This works well, but is time-consuming. Follow the instructions in the grinder instruction booklet.
• Use a special grinder cleaner. This comes in the form of granules that you pour into the hopper and which then get ground like coffee beans, dislodging any coffee particles and absorbing any oily residues. Although this is a

specially designed, neutral product, you should discard the first set of coffee grounds produced after using this cleaner.

MOVING BURR

FIXED BURR

SOLUTION 1 : REMOVE THE BURR

SOLUTION 2 : CLEANING GRANULES

How often? Once for every 55 lb of coffee ground. The frequency can be increased or decreased depending on the roast level of the beans used.

WATER!

Water is composed of two chemical elements, hydrogen and oxygen (H_2O), but the water we use is never in this pure form. On its travels it takes up minerals and trace elements whose chemical properties affect the taste of the coffee. So it is important for your water to meet certain criteria.

Whatever the coffee preparation method used, the water has to extract the aromatic compounds from the grounds without itself affecting the flavor of the drink. An espresso consists of approximately 88 percent water, and a filter coffee more than 98 percent. But take note: some waters are better than others . . .

88% WATER

98% WATER

To make the grade, water has to be:

Neutral-tasting
Waters don't all taste the same. The flavor varies depending on the proportions of minerals and trace elements they contain, as well as the amount of chlorine (in the case of tap water). To make a good coffee, you need to use fresh, pure water that is free of intrusive odors.

Capable of revealing the flavor of the coffee
The minerals contained in the water can be isolated by heating the water to 350°F and allowing it to evaporate. These mineral salts and other trace elements affect the taste of the water and its ability to extract the aromatic compounds from the coffee. According to taste tests organized by the SCAA (Specialty Coffee Association of America), the level of dry residue should be around 150 mg/L for a balanced cup of coffee.

Neither too hard nor too soft
For coffee, the measure that matters is the temporary hardness, or carbonate hardness (KH), which must be between 3 and 5 degrees KH. However, the permanent hardness also has to be lower than the temporary hardness to avoid clogging and to ensure the right mineral balance to give a good-tasting coffee. If the water is too hard, espresso machines, electric coffee makers and kettles become encrusted with limescale on the inside. If the water is too soft, the KH no longer serves as a buffer cushioning variations in pH levels, so there is a risk that the machine parts will become corroded.

IN A NUTSHELL

If the water is too hard, the coffee machine will become encrusted with limescale.

If the water is too soft, the boiler will corrode.

All in all, limescale encrustation is the preferable option.

A QUICK CHEMISTRY LESSON

If all this is not quite crystal clear yet, don't panic!
Here are a few simple pointers on the subject of water hardness and pH.

What is water hardness?

When you bring water to a boil in a pan, the temporary hardness (KH) is lost and shows up instead as white limescale deposits around the sides of the pan. This is because bicarbonates of calcium and magnesium in the water are precipitated out as carbonates on application of heat.

Permanent hardness is the hardness that remains in the water after boiling. It refers to the concentration of sulfates of calcium (gypsum) and magnesium.

The temporary hardness and permanent hardness can be added together to give the total hardness (GH). This is the figure usually indicated by the water company.

Total hardness (GH) = temporary hardness (KH) + permanent hardness. Hardness is expressed in "German degrees": °dH.

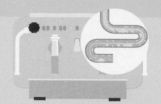

GYPSUM PASSES THROUGH PIPING, SO IT IS NOT A PROBLEM FOR COFFEE MACHINES BUT IT DOES IMPART A PARTICULAR TASTE TO THE WATER.

TOTAL HARDNESS =
PERMANENT HARDNESS + TEMPORARY HARDNESS

GYPSUM STAYS IN THE WATER AFTER BOILING

CALCIUM SHOWS UP AS WHITE DEPOSITS ON THE SIDES OF THE PAN AFTER BOILING

What about the pH?

The pH (potential of hydrogen) is used to define, on a scale of 1 to 14, whether water is acidic, alkaline, or neutral:

- If the pH < 7: the water is acidic.
- If the pH > 7: the water is alkaline.
- If the pH = 7: the water is neutral.

The mineral content of the water affects its pH; the higher the mineral content, the higher its pH level; the softer the water, the more acidic it is.

To protect machines from corrosion, the pH should not be allowed to go below 6.5.

TESTING YOUR WATER!

You can measure the properties of your water (KH and pH) using a water test kit for aquarium owners. Some espresso machine manufacturers also sell kits for measuring the hardness of your water yourself.

ACIDIC   NEUTRAL   ALKALINE

CHOOSING YOUR WATER

Choosing the right water for your coffee is an easy and effective way
of improving its quality.

Bottled water

Mineral water or spring water is not the most economical nor the most eco-friendly solution, but it allows you to choose a water that is well suited to the type of coffee you want to brew. For espresso, you need to take into account the hardness of the water and its pH level. For gentle methods, there is no particular requirement in terms of machine maintenance (except in the case of electric coffee makers); the choice of water depends instead on the desired result in the cup.

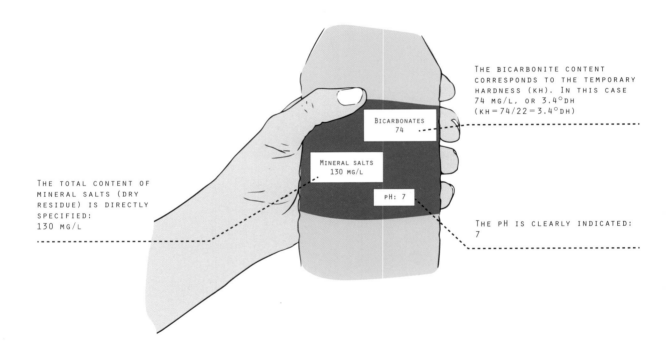

THE BICARBONITE CONTENT CORRESPONDS TO THE TEMPORARY HARDNESS (KH). IN THIS CASE 74 MG/L, OR 3.4°DH (KH=74/22=3.4°DH)

BICARBONATES 74

MINERAL SALTS 130 MG/L

PH: 7

THE TOTAL CONTENT OF MINERAL SALTS (DRY RESIDUE) IS DIRECTLY SPECIFIED: 130 MG/L

THE PH IS CLEARLY INDICATED: 7

MINERAL WATER *vs* SPRING WATER

These designations, used for bottled waters, are controlled appellations. Both describe drinkable water derived from untreated groundwater. Mineral water is a spring water that exhibits particular recognized properties (including many therapeutic benefits). Its composition is more stable over time, but it is not necessarily higher in minerals than a spring water.

Filtered water

Unless you live in an area where tap water does not require treatment, water from your faucet needs to be filtered to improve its properties.

If the KH of the tap water = 3 to 5°dH
A simple activated carbon filter can help eliminate any intrusive odors, such as the smell of chlorine.

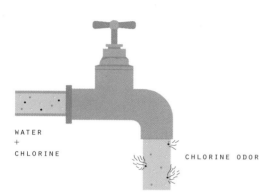

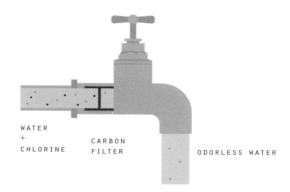

If the KH of the tap water > 5°dH
Use a more elaborate filter cartridge with an extra ion-exchange resin phase to reduce calcium (or gypsum in some areas). These filters come in the form of a cartridge that is placed in the water reservoir of an espresso machine, or in a water filter pitcher. Whatever the case, be sure to check that the pH of the filtered water does not go below the 6.5 threshold for espresso machines and other electric coffee makers, as this could lead to corrosion and damage to the machine.

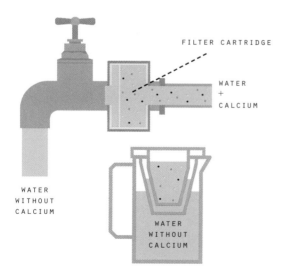

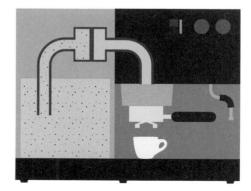

YOUR PERFECT CUP

Whether consumed at the counter, at the table, or on the move, coffee can be served in and drunk from all sorts of vessels. Cups, glasses, and mugs play a big part in determining the final outcome.

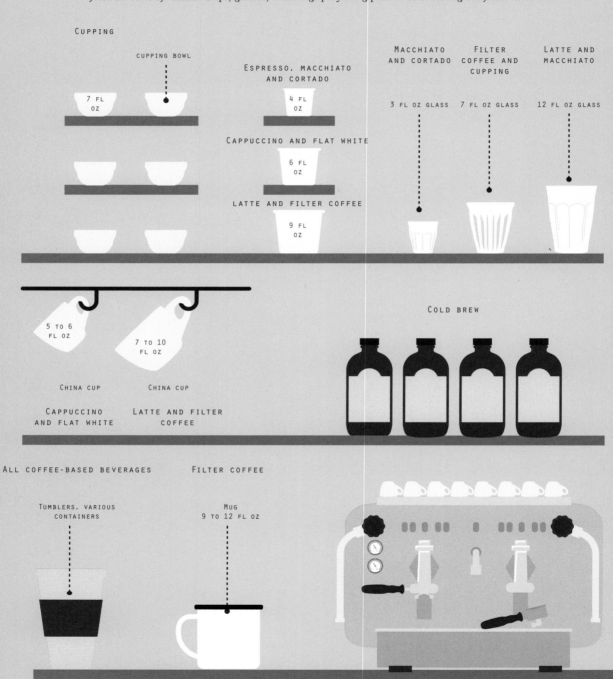

CUPPING

CUPPING BOWL

7 FL OZ

ESPRESSO, MACCHIATO AND CORTADO

4 FL OZ

CAPPUCCINO AND FLAT WHITE

6 FL OZ

LATTE AND FILTER COFFEE

9 FL OZ

MACCHIATO AND CORTADO

3 FL OZ GLASS

FILTER COFFEE AND CUPPING

7 FL OZ GLASS

LATTE AND MACCHIATO

12 FL OZ GLASS

5 TO 6 FL OZ

7 TO 10 FL OZ

CHINA CUP

CAPPUCCINO AND FLAT WHITE

CHINA CUP

LATTE AND FILTER COFFEE

COLD BREW

ALL COFFEE-BASED BEVERAGES

TUMBLERS, VARIOUS CONTAINERS

FILTER COFFEE

MUG
9 TO 12 FL OZ

THE ESPRESSO CUP

When serving espresso, a china cup will always be the most suitable vessel,
but to deliver the flavors of the coffee most effectively, it needs to satisfy certain criteria.

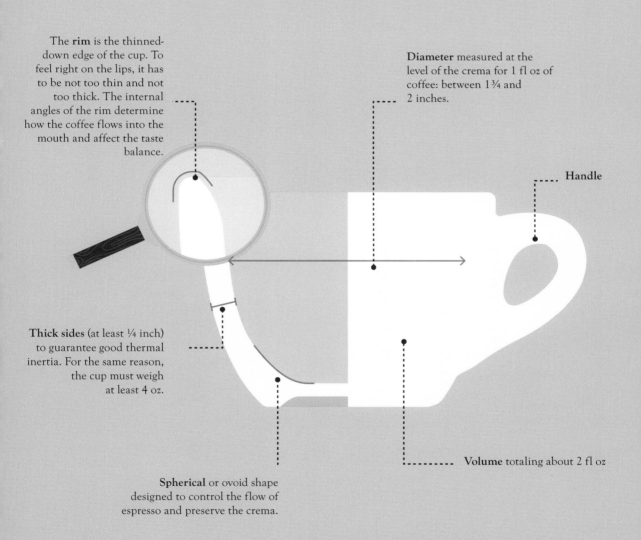

The **rim** is the thinned-down edge of the cup. To feel right on the lips, it has to be not too thin and not too thick. The internal angles of the rim determine how the coffee flows into the mouth and affect the taste balance.

Diameter measured at the level of the crema for 1 fl oz of coffee: between 1¾ and 2 inches.

Handle

Thick sides (at least ¼ inch) to guarantee good thermal inertia. For the same reason, the cup must weigh at least 4 oz.

Spherical or ovoid shape designed to control the flow of espresso and preserve the crema.

Volume totaling about 2 fl oz

THICK

FULL-BODIED

SYRUPY

WITH CREMA

EXPLOSIVE

HIGH PRESSURE
(9 BAR)

STRONG

CONCENTRATED

11.5%
COFFEE

QUICK TO
PREPARE

88.5%
WATER

DRUNK
QUICKLY

1 FL OZ

ESPRESSO

To produce an espresso, high pressure is used to extract the aromatic compounds from the coffee.

Short and speedy

An espresso is a short coffee (between ½ fl oz and 2 fl oz), brewed a cup at a time. This method differs from others in that the hot water is under pressure and percolates rapidly (for between 20 and 30 seconds) through the grounds to extract the oils and other aromatic compounds from the coffee.

Small yet potent

This beverage is characterized by the presence of a surface foam, called the crema in Italy. This emulsion is composed of the smallest particles of ground coffee (known as the "fines"), water, coffee oil (caffeol), and carbon dioxide (CO_2). A cup of espresso has a powerful, explosive taste with plenty of body. An espresso is on average ten times more concentrated than a filter coffee.

THE LONG HISTORY OF A SHORT COFFEE

This highly fashionable brewing method was invented in 1820, the brainchild of a Frenchman,
Louis Bernard Rabaut, before being popularized and refined by the Italians.

1820 **1855** **1884**

The idea of using steam to force hot water through dark-roasted, finely ground coffee beans came from a Frenchman, Louis Bernard Rabaut.

This concept was put into practice by another Frenchman, Édouard Loysel de Santais, for the first Universal Exhibition in Paris in 1855, in the form of his hydrostatic percolator, capable of delivering large volumes of coffee, tea, or even beer in record time.

At the Turin exhibition in 1884, the Italian entrepreneur Angelo Moriondo exhibited his "steam machinery for the economic and instantaneous confection of coffee beverage," for which he was awarded the bronze medal. At the time it wasn't yet known as an espresso machine, but several such machines were produced for use in his family's hotels and restaurants.

A FAIR EXCHANGE

It may have been the Italians who refined and set the standards for espresso, but, contrary to popular belief, the famous drink nevertheless had its roots in France. It is worth noting, though, that it was following that same Universal Exhibition in Paris in 1855 that the sixty-two Bordeaux "crus" were awarded their official classification, when the fact is that wine had itself been imported into Gaul by the Romans.

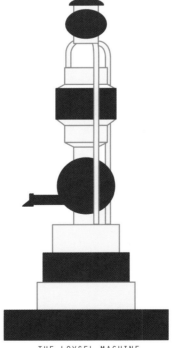

THE LOYSEL MACHINE

A SPOT OF VOCABULARY

The term "percolator" comes from the English verb "percolate," itself derived from the Latin verb "percolare," meaning "to pass through, to filter." The term "hydrostatic" indicates that the extraction pressure is produced by the weight of a column of water (1 bar for every 10 meters).

1 FL OZ

1901

The year 1901 saw the arrival of the Tipo Gigante by Luigi Bezzera, and of its near identical twin, the Ideale by Desiderio Pavoni, the first real espresso machines with a portafilter that brewed individual cups.

1947

In 1947, Achille Gaggia and his lever espresso machine enabled the pressure to be raised from 1.5 to 9 bar, resulting in the production of crema, which hadn't appeared before that time because there wasn't sufficient pressure.

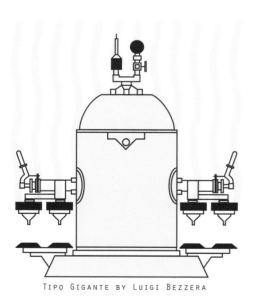

TIPO GIGANTE BY LUIGI BEZZERA

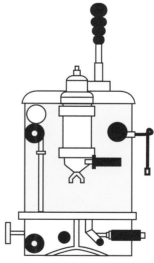

GAGGIA LEVER MACHINE

DESIGNED TO BE BREWED AND CONSUMED RAPIDLY

Quick to order, quick to prepare, and quick to drink, the espresso was born of the need to save time. In fact, Luigi Bezzera developed his Tipo Gigante in order to reduce the amount of time his employees were spending on their breaks! It is often said that an espresso should be consumed within four minutes of brewing.

ESPRESSO: THE TASTING EXPERIENCE

To properly appreciate an espresso, you need, above all, to taste it and savor it as you would do with wine, to name the sensations you experience when you breathe in its fragrance and when you focus on the responses of your taste buds and the flavors left in your mouth, right down to the final note. Senses ready, get set, go!

The ritual

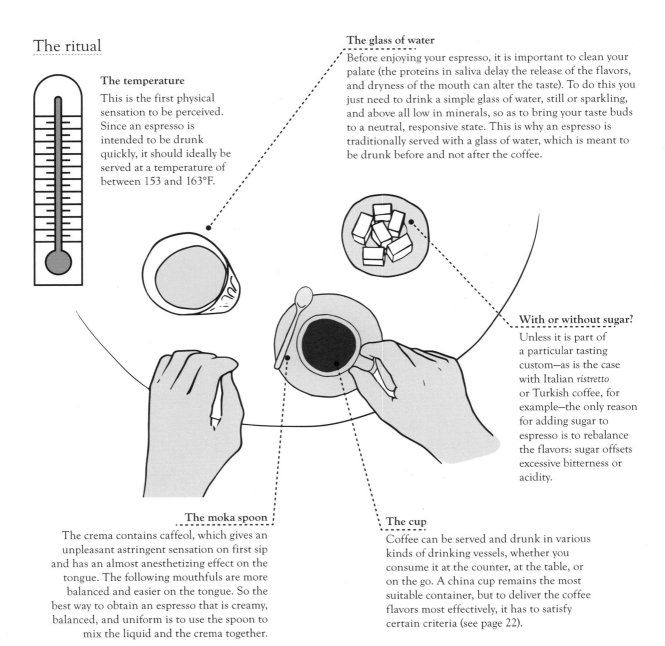

The temperature
This is the first physical sensation to be perceived. Since an espresso is intended to be drunk quickly, it should ideally be served at a temperature of between 153 and 163°F.

The glass of water
Before enjoying your espresso, it is important to clean your palate (the proteins in saliva delay the release of the flavors, and dryness of the mouth can alter the taste). To do this you just need to drink a simple glass of water, still or sparkling, and above all low in minerals, so as to bring your taste buds to a neutral, responsive state. This is why an espresso is traditionally served with a glass of water, which is meant to be drunk before and not after the coffee.

With or without sugar?
Unless it is part of a particular tasting custom—as is the case with Italian *ristretto* or Turkish coffee, for example—the only reason for adding sugar to espresso is to rebalance the flavors: sugar offsets excessive bitterness or acidity.

The moka spoon
The crema contains caffeol, which gives an unpleasant astringent sensation on first sip and has an almost anesthetizing effect on the tongue. The following mouthfuls are more balanced and easier on the tongue. So the best way to obtain an espresso that is creamy, balanced, and uniform is to use the spoon to mix the liquid and the crema together.

The cup
Coffee can be served and drunk in various kinds of drinking vessels, whether you consume it at the counter, at the table, or on the go. A china cup remains the most suitable container, but to deliver the coffee flavors most effectively, it has to satisfy certain criteria (see page 22).

Sensations

The crema

The crema is the only visual indicator of an espresso. Its coloring, thickness, and streakiness are not enough to reveal its quality, but they are good indicators of the freshness and roast level of the coffee. If, despite being correctly prepared, the crema is very (overly) pale, doesn't cover the entire surface of the coffee, or vanishes before four minutes have elapsed, there is a good chance the beans were not roasted for long enough or were not fresh. The crema alone doesn't make the espresso, but it does play an important part.

Light crema may reveal an excellent espresso.

Streaked crema with pretty reddish hues may well conceal a coffee with unbalanced flavors.

Sparse crema may indicate an issue with the coffee beans (roasting, freshness).

The nose

As with a wine, one talks about the "nose" of an espresso. The odors that emanate from it must only contain positive notes, such as odors of nuts (peanuts, hazelnuts …), of spices (anise, cinnamon …), of fruits (red fruits, peaches …), or of flowers (jasmine, rose …). Woody, smoky, or tobacco notes would tend to be considered negative.

The aromas

While the odors are detected directly by the nose, the aromas, meanwhile, are experienced by retronasal olfaction, from the first sip to the finish.

Like the nose, the aromas borne by the volatile molecules can be fruity, spicy, or floral. However, a coffee's odors and aromas are not necessarily identical. With specialty coffees, the aromas are now considered an integral part of the tasting experience. Retronasal olfaction enables us to gauge the aromatic complexity, a measure of the finest coffees.

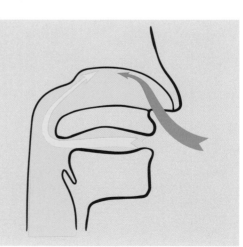

ESPRESSO: THE TASTING EXPERIENCE

The body

The body refers to the substance or consistency of the coffee. Viscosity is an important feature of espresso, which is ten times more concentrated than a filter coffee. The high pressure causes the oils to emulsify, giving a sense of thickness in the mouth. One might refer to an espresso as being full-bodied, thick, viscous, or syrupy, as opposed to watery, thin, flat, or light …

The texture of a coffee is composed of sensations derived from the sense of touch, which are conveyed by the trigeminal nerve.

FULL-BODIED ESPRESSO

THIN/FLAT ESPRESSO

Astringency

This is one of the most unpleasant physical sensations you might experience in an espresso. It involves a mechanical tensing of the mucous membranes, accompanied by a feeling of roughness and dryness, which is amplified by the bitterness and acidity.

The taste

Of the five primary tastes conveyed by the nonvolatile molecules that are detected by the taste buds, those that dominate in the case of coffee are sourness, sweetness, and bitterness.

SEE NEXT PAGE FOR ALL THE COFFEE TASTES

Primary tastes under the microscope

Here is a guide to help you recognize the different flavors you may encounter in coffee, and especially to help you tell the difference between sourness and bitterness. The illustrations give an example of a food or drink that exhibits that particular flavor, to enable you to identify the flavor we are referring to.

BITTERNESS

Our innate rejection of bitterness is thought to be an age-old natural defense designed to protect us from natural poisons, most of which have a bitter taste. Incidentally, the bitterness in coffee is primarily due to caffeine, a natural insecticide, and also to trigonelline, another alkaloid, which is derived from vitamin B_3.

GRAPEFRUIT

CHICORY

SOURNESS

This is a sensation that strikes you right away, often from the first mouthful. It may take different forms. The experience of sourness varies from one person to another because when we taste coffee, it is our own personal saliva-acid combination that we perceive.

LIME

Citric acid develops in beans cultivated at high altitude. It is a sign of having been freshly harvested.

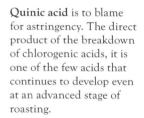

TONIC WATER

Quinic acid is to blame for astringency. The direct product of the breakdown of chlorogenic acids, it is one of the few acids that continues to develop even at an advanced stage of roasting.

APPLE

Malic acid, with its metallic taste, is typical of some coffees from East Africa (Burundi, Rwanda). But it can also be an indicator of a premature harvest.

COLA

Phosphoric acid, which, unlike the others, is inorganic, is characteristic of the Kenyan varieties SL28 and SL34.

VINEGAR

Acetic acid, when present in excessive quantities, gives a tartness that is deemed negative. Like quinic acid, it continues to develop even at an advanced stage of roasting.

WHAT ABOUT SALTINESS?

Only certain coffees exhibit salty flavors: monsoon coffees, for example (see page 113).

SWEETNESS

Sugar gives sweetness and makes the sourness more palatable.

A BALANCED ESPRESSO IS A WELL-CRAFTED MIXTURE OF SOUR AND BITTER TASTES

In France, coffee is regarded as a bitter product. Over time, the bitterness in espresso has declined, accompanied by an increase in sourness, which brings fruity aromas and flavors to the coffee. It lends vivacity and freshness, makes you salivate, and supports the aromas and the finish. So sourness is a positive attribute, provided it is not overpowering. Like sweetness, bitterness affects one's perception of sourness. So these two tastes, which are naturally opposed, are indispensable when it comes to preparing a balanced, that is, slightly sour, espresso.

TASTING

*The concept of "good" is cultural, personal, and subjective. It is closely linked to the idea of pleasure felt.
An espresso may display no shortcomings, but nevertheless be boring, conjuring no response whatsoever.
The all-important factor, more than rules and other tasting criteria, is for the experience to be pleasurable.*

In the mouth

Espresso tasting can be divided into three phases: beginning, middle, and end. Each phase may be dominated by one flavor: for example, a sour beginning, a balanced middle, and a slightly bitter finish. Ideally, the finish, also known as the "length on the palate" or aftertaste, should offer aromas rather than flavors. Each coffee has its own tasting curve (rising, falling, straight …).

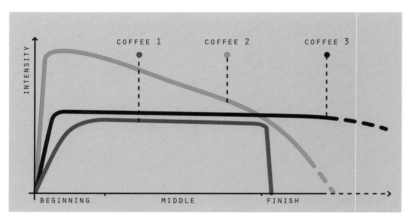

- COFFEE 1: THE FLAVOR INTENSITY INCREASES GRADUALLY AND DROPS ABRUPTLY: THERE IS ALMOST NO FINISH.
- COFFEE 2: QUITE A VIOLENT BEGINNING, FOLLOWED BY A GRADUALLY DIMINISHING MIDDLE AND FINISH.
- COFFEE 3: A VERY "STRAIGHT" COFFEE. HERE NO SINGLE PHASE DOMINATES OVER THE OTHERS. THE MOUTH FINISH IS LONG AND LASTS FOR SEVERAL MINUTES.

The coffee's flavor

All the sensations identified and analyzed, added together, define the flavor of the coffee. The more harmonious these perceptions, the more balanced the espresso.

 A GOOD ESPRESSO
MIGHT BE DESCRIBED AS:

Complex:	Offering a multitude of harmonious positive sensations.
Clean:	Having no apparent major fault.
Sweet:	A pleasant coffee offering sweetness and mellow aromas.
Smooth:	Sweet and slightly tangy.
Full-bodied:	Having a nice mouthfeel.
Balanced:	The tastes blend well together and give a slightly tangy coffee.

A BAD ESPRESSO MIGHT BE DESCRIBED AS:

Acrid:	A tart coffee (see acetic acid) with an unpleasant acidity.
Harsh:	A rough coffee giving a sensation of coarseness in the mouth.
Woody:	A negative attribute for an espresso. The woody aroma is due to poor storage of the green coffee and/or an unsuitable roast profile.
Rancid:	Rancid taste due to being stored poorly or for too long, often after overroasting.
Bitter:	Bitterness, when excessive, is considered a flaw.
Old crop:	A coffee lacking freshness, rancid, woody, with odors reminiscent of hessian (see page 134).

EXAMPLE OF A TASTING FORM

NAME: El Salvador Finca La Fany

VARIETY: Red Bourbon

DRYING: washed and sun-dried

ROAST DATE: 04/14/16

TASTING DATE: 04/30/16

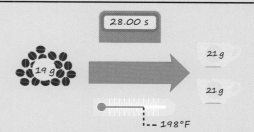

NOSE

POSITIVES
- ✓ NUTS
- RED FRUIT
- TROPICAL FRUIT
- STONE FRUIT
- CITRUS
- VEGETAL
- FLORAL
- SPICE

NEGATIVES
- SMOKY
- GRASSY
- WOODY
- BURNT

NOTES : almonds

AROMAS

POSITIVES
- ✓ NUTS
- ✓ RED FRUIT
- TROPICAL FRUIT
- STONE FRUIT
- CITRUS
- VEGETAL
- FLORAL
- SPICE

NEGATIVES
- SMOKY
- GRASSY
- WOODY
- BURNT

NOTES : black currant, hazelnut

BODY

1   2   ✗   3   4   5

CLEAN CUP

1   2   3   ✗   4   5

BALANCE

1   ✗ 2   3   4   5

LENGTH OF FINISH

1   2   3   4 ✗   5

CREMA

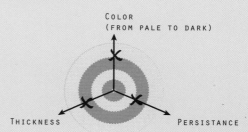

COLOR
(FROM PALE TO DARK)

THICKNESS   PERSISTANCE

PRIMARY TASTES

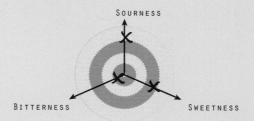

SOURNESS

BITTERNESS   SWEETNESS

FLAVOR, GENERAL MOUTHFEEL

Lively espresso. Sourness brings freshness and depth. Quite creamy. Lingering and pleasant finish. Slightly lacking in balance. An interesting espresso that is pleasurable to drink.

THE ESPRESSO MACHINE

Types of machines

Domestic machine

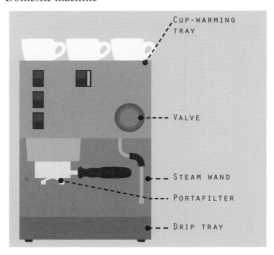

CUP-WARMING TRAY

VALVE

STEAM WAND

PORTAFILTER

DRIP TRAY

Professional machine

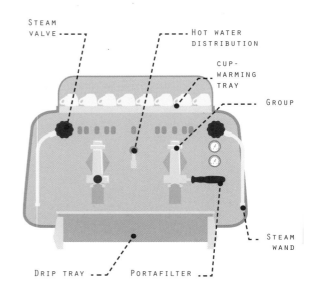

STEAM VALVE

HOT WATER DISTRIBUTION

CUP-WARMING TRAY

GROUP

STEAM WAND

DRIP TRAY

PORTAFILTER

GOOD VIBRATIONS...

Domestic machines work on the principle of an oscillating piston, which unfortunately emits vibrations and is very noisy in operation. But it also has some positive attributes. Though noisy, the low cost and small size of the pump have made the domestic espresso machine accessible to all.

Filters and portafilters

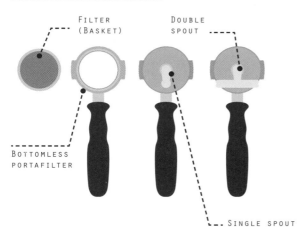

FILTER (BASKET)

DOUBLE SPOUT

BOTTOMLESS PORTAFILTER

SINGLE SPOUT

THERE'S CREMA, AND THEN THERE'S *CREMA*: THE TRICK WITH PRESSURIZED FILTERS

Entry-level espresso machines aimed at the general public are often equipped with pressurized filters. These are baskets with just a single hole in them, rather than a conventional basket. The idea is to spare the user from having to buy a grinder, because rather than carefully adapting the grind to achieve the ideal pressure and give a perfect crema, these filters use this "technical trick" to create artificial pressure, masking the true percolation speed of the coffee. The result is a foam consisting of rather large bubbles on your espresso, regardless of the size of the grind, but the flavor result is far from satisfactory for a true coffee lover ...

Machine models

The traditional machine is the most widely used. It is also known as an injection machine. Designed in 1961 by Carlo Ernesto Valente and named the E 61 (E for Eclipse, 1961 being the year of a total solar eclipse) for the company FAEMA, which set the standard for espresso machines for some forty years.

The lever machine is the forerunner of the motorized pump machine. It is still widely used in southern Italy.

TRADITIONAL MACHINE

PRINCIPLE:
An electromechanical pump injects water under pressure to produce the extraction.

USE:
Professional or domestic.

PROS:
Multipurpose, good-quality brew.

CONS:
Need to have a good understanding of espresso extraction to achieve a good result.

LEVER MACHINE

PRINCIPLE:
It uses the same principle as a bicycle pump to create pressure; the force exerted by the barista on the lever is transmitted to a piston (in some cases spring-loaded).

USE:
Professional or domestic.

PROS:
Attractive-looking, flavorsome *ristretto*, silent (no electric pump!), strengthens your arm muscles!

CONS:
Not very practical, not really suitable for long espressos.

A compromise between a traditional machine and a capsule machine, the automatic machine leaves the choice of coffee up to you.

Designed for home users wanting a way of making an espresso quickly, easily, and regularly, the capsule machine also appeals to a lot of catering professionals.

AUTOMATIC MACHINE

PRINCIPLE:
This machine is equipped with an integrated grinder. There are various preset programs to choose from; you just have to press the appropriate button.

USE:
Domestic.

PROS:
Easy to use (although some menus can get very complex!), possible to use coffee beans.

CONS:
Coffee quality leaves room for improvement (lack of body, aromas not fully revealed …), less reliable than a traditional machine, high purchase cost.

CAPSULE MACHINE

PRINCIPLE:
You insert a pre-dosed capsule into the machine, push a button, and a preset program extracts the coffee.

USE:
Domestic.

PROS:
Simple to use, consistent result in the cup, machine is inexpensive to purchase.

CONS:
Limited choice of coffee, cost per cup, coffee of mediocre quality, barista cannot influence the brew other than the length in the cup, not eco-friendly.

CHOOSING YOUR MACHINE

There are several styles of espresso machine available, and such a plethora of products that it is difficult to know where to start. The espresso machine you choose depends first and foremost on how much coffee you need to brew each day. This should help give you a better idea …

From the bakery to the large restaurant

The brewing group of an espresso machine is the part into which the portafilter engages; it is the part that connects the water reservoir to the portafilter. The number of groups is chosen to suit the amount of coffee to be brewed. Home espresso machines only have a single group, whereas professional machines can have up to four groups, and machines with even more groups can be made to order.

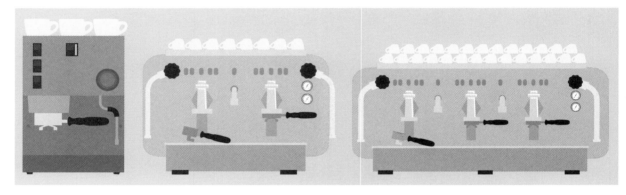

SINGLE GROUP   TWO GROUPS   THREE OR MORE GROUPS

< 2 LB OF COFFEE/DAY

COFFEE CORNERS
IN SHOPS AND
BAKERIES

2 TO 15 LB OF COFFEE/DAY

COFFEE SHOP,
SMALL RESTAURANTS

>15 LB OF COFFEE/DAY

CAFÉS, LARGE RESTAURANTS

For those who can't decide: the prosumer

Machines intended for commercial settings are made using more reliable and durable components to enable them to cope with intensive, continuous use. In the early 2000s, private consumers who wanted to have their own high-performance machine at home started purchasing single-group professional machines, generally secondhand. In response to this new demand, manufacturers started developing semiprofessional machines known as "prosumer" (a contraction of "professional" and "consumer") machines, which combine technical solutions and professional components in small espresso machines for domestic use.

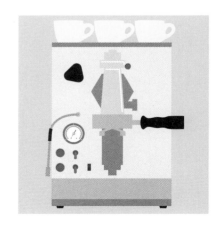

A machine to suit everyone

The latte art geek
You're a coffee geek who likes to practice latte art at home. A single-group semiprofessional (*prosumer*) machine with a heat exchanger will suit your needs. You can have steam whenever you want it, and can brew one cappuccino after another to enable you to practice your ephemeral art.

The fan of terroir
You're fascinated by the amazing diversity of coffees offered by the countless terroirs, or coffee-producing regions, around the world. A single-group, single-boiler machine does a good job of conveying all the nuances and aromatic complexity of the best coffee beans. The fact that this machine does not offer steam on demand is not a problem, especially if you're not big on milky coffee, and only occasionally prepare this if you happen to have guests visiting.

The barista
A two-group espresso machine is good for use in a small coffee shop. The machine needs to operate at a stable, accurate temperature, and provide plenty of steam power, enough to cope with the high demand for milky drinks.

The office coffee klatch
An automatic machine is probably best for the office. This machine, which is very easy to use, can be operated individually by ten or so different people throughout the day, and allows each of them to select their desired program. With its integrated coffee grinder, it uses coffee beans, rather than capsules, making it an environmentally friendly choice. The high purchase price may be less of a problem since it's usually purchased by companies for use by employees.

The vacation home
A capsule machine may be the best option, since it may only get use a few weeks out of the year. It's relatively inexpensive and the amount of coffee one needs to buy (as capsules) can be tailored to the exact amount of coffee consumed. The intuitive operation and speed with which you can prepare coffees are useful in a house where there is a lot of coming and going.

MAINTAINING YOUR MACHINE

You won't get a good espresso if you don't have a spotless machine.
Some tips for keeping your machine in pristine condition.

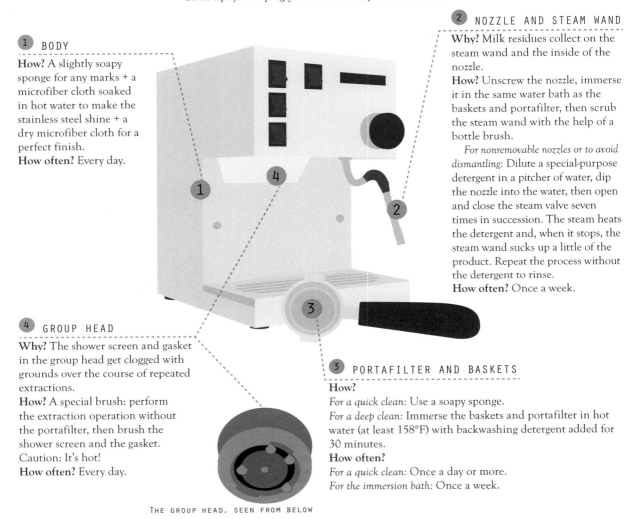

① BODY

How? A slightly soapy sponge for any marks + a microfiber cloth soaked in hot water to make the stainless steel shine + a dry microfiber cloth for a perfect finish.
How often? Every day.

② NOZZLE AND STEAM WAND

Why? Milk residues collect on the steam wand and the inside of the nozzle.
How? Unscrew the nozzle, immerse it in the same water bath as the baskets and portafilter, then scrub the steam wand with the help of a bottle brush.

For nonremovable nozzles or to avoid dismantling: Dilute a special-purpose detergent in a pitcher of water, dip the nozzle into the water, then open and close the steam valve seven times in succession. The steam heats the detergent and, when it stops, the steam wand sucks up a little of the product. Repeat the process without the detergent to rinse.
How often? Once a week.

④ GROUP HEAD

Why? The shower screen and gasket in the group head get clogged with grounds over the course of repeated extractions.
How? A special brush: perform the extraction operation without the portafilter, then brush the shower screen and the gasket. Caution: It's hot!
How often? Every day.

THE GROUP HEAD, SEEN FROM BELOW

③ PORTAFILTER AND BASKETS

How?
For a quick clean: Use a soapy sponge.
For a deep clean: Immerse the baskets and portafilter in hot water (at least 158°F) with backwashing detergent added for 30 minutes.
How often?
For a quick clean: Once a day or more.
For the immersion bath: Once a week.

BACKWASHING FOR MACHINES WITH A DEPRESSURIZATION SYSTEM

Why? This innovation makes it possible to remove the portafilter from the group just after the extraction of the coffee. But this causes grounds to work their way up inside the group, fouling the internal circuit and producing a rancid taste.
How? Backwashing with a special detergent: Place a blind filter (i.e., one with no holes) in the portafilter, place the dose of detergent (between 3 and 9 g) in the blind filter, fasten the portafilter to the group head, and run five cycles (run for 5 seconds / stop for 15 seconds). Remove the portafilter, run a rinse cycle to flush the detergent out of the group, and rinse the blind filter. Repeat the operation without detergent to rinse the circuit. The first coffee after cleaning should be discarded.
How often? Once a week in a domestic setting; at the end of each day in a professional setting.

DETERGENT IN THE FILTER

HOW IT WORKS

The principle of operation of an espresso machine is the same for all, regardless of the model. A boiler, usually equipped with a heating element, is used to produce hot water, which is then pressurized with the aid of a pump and forced through the coffee grounds.

TEMPERATURE 198°F + PRESSURE 9 BAR = GOOD EXTRACTION OF THE AROMAS AND FLAVORS

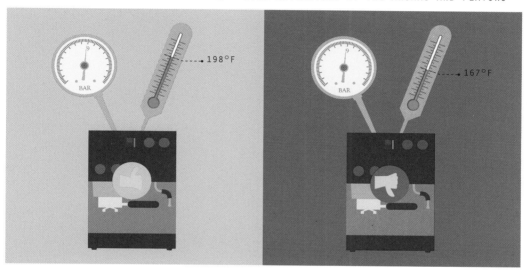

SO THE AIM IS ALWAYS TO MAINTAIN A TEMPERATURE OF 198°F (SEE PAGES 48–49)

It is, technically speaking, easy to maintain stable pressure. But temperature is another matter. It is tricky enough to keep the temperature stable during the time it takes to pull one shot of coffee, let alone when you are pulling several shots in succession. Any variations in temperature then cause inconsistency in the taste of the coffee.

HIGH PRESSURE = A QUALITY SHOT?

Some espresso machine manufacturers offer pressures of up to 18 bar, suggesting this improves the quality of the extraction. The optimum pressure for espresso is 8 to 10 bar; if it is > 10 bar, there is a risk of overextraction of the grounds, yielding a bitter coffee. Professional machines are set to 9 bar by installers, and serious domestic machines come with a built-in pressure limiter in case the pump has a tendency to become overzealous. So don't let yourself be impressed by high numbers!

BUT WHAT IS PRESSURE?

Pressure is a force that acts on a surface. Its unit of measurement is the bar, with 1 bar equal to the pressure exerted by a mass of 1 kg on an area of 1 cm^2. We find examples of different pressure levels in daily life: atmospheric pressure, that is, the pressure of the air that surrounds us (approximately 1 bar); submarine pressure, which increases by 1 bar for every 10 m (33 ft) you go down; car tire pressure (2 bar); public works water pressure (3 bar), etc.

HOW TO MAINTAIN
A STABLE TEMPERATURE

Espresso machines are fitted with one or two boilers to heat the water.
Boilers are categorized according to volume, and their job is to increase the temperature of the water.
While nearly all boiler mechanisms use an electric element (nowadays, gas models are
generally only used in countries that do not have a stable, effective public electrical network),
there are various different techniques for obtaining both hot water and steam at the same time.

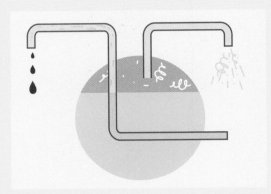

COFFEE MODE   OR   STEAM MODE

Heat exchanger

First used in 1961 on the FAEMA E 61, the heat
exchanger works on the same principle as the bain-
marie. A single boiler with a capacity of several pints
is heated to 270°F to produce steam and heats the
water entering via the heat exchanger, which is simply
a thin, submerged tube. The heat exchanger receives
cold water from the water reservoir or the water
mains, and brings it to the right temperature for
extracting the coffee drink from the grounds.

Single boiler

The system could not be simpler. In coffee mode, the boiler provides
an ideal temperature of 198°F for making espresso. In steam mode,
the temperature is increased by about 122°F in order to generate the
steam to froth the milk for a cappuccino, for example.

Double boiler

This is the most advanced technology, first employed by
La Marzocco in 1970. This works on the principle that you
have one boiler dedicated to coffee brewing and the other to
steam generation.

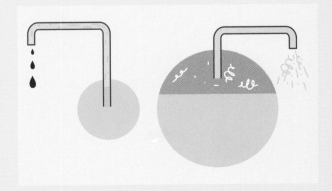

WHAT ABOUT THERMOBLOCK MACHINES?

The thermoblock is a narrow coil equipped with a heating element that flash-heats the water passing through it. The benefit with this method is that the heating time is massively reduced. The machine is ready to use in two to three minutes, compared to at least thirty minutes for a boiler machine. However, its lack of thermal stability means it only tends to be used in entry-level domestic machines and capsule machines. Not recommended, then!

IN A NUTSHELL

	SINGLE BOILER	HEAT EXCHANGER	DOUBLE BOILER
FOR	Domestic espresso machines	The majority of prosumer and professional machines	The top-performing prosumer and professional machines
THE +	Well-designed technical solution, highly efficient in terms of extraction, with a stable temperature.	• Simultaneous coffee and steam functions. • Its small capacity means the infusion water is constantly renewed.	The fact that it has two independent boilers means you don't have to settle for a compromise in terms of steam power versus extraction temperature (extremely stable).
THE −	• Impossible to generate steam while brewing an espresso. • You have to wait several minutes before you can produce steam, and wait for the water to cool down again afterward if you want to brew more coffees.	• The temperature of the water heated in this way may vary by several degrees on exit from the group head. • The extraction temperature is dependent on that of the steam boiler.	The cost, as some parts are duplicated (boilers, heating elements, etc.).
TAKE NOTE	Opt for a brass boiler, rather than an aluminum one, with a capacity of at least 10 fl oz for optimum performance (best thermal inertia).	The heat exchanger's small volume makes it vulnerable to limescale.	The water in the coffee boiler is refreshed less frequently than in a heat exchanger, but this no longer poses a health issue thanks to improvements in the quality of public water and filtration systems.

DIGITAL TEMPERATURE CONTROL

This technology was launched on the market in 2005 by La Marzocco in response to an initiative by David Schomer, pioneer of specialty coffee and founder of Espresso Vivace in Seattle. Together they developed electronic temperature controllers, known as PID (proportional, integral, and derivative) controllers, for espresso machine boilers. This system offers better thermal stability and the facility to accurately regulate the extraction temperature with the aid of a digital control panel. This technology is becoming increasingly common in prosumer and professional machines.

THE BARISTA'S ROUTINE

These are the actions the barista performs over and over each day.

SETTING THE MACHINE TIMER

Not all machines come with a function for setting the start-up time. The other way is to use a small timer plugged directly into the power socket, which is set to wake up the coffee machine before the rest of the household.

In the case of professional machines, it is more environmentally friendly to leave them constantly switched on, because it takes them a very long time to heat up. Some machines offer an eco-friendly, money-saving standby function that allows the temperature to drop slightly during the night.

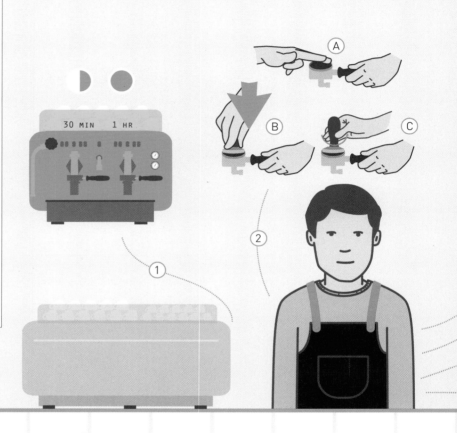

① Warm-up time

All parts of the espresso machine have to be hot. This takes at least thirty minutes for a domestic machine and one hour for a commercial one. Don't go by the light! It indicates the temperature of the water, not of the machine itself.
Note: The portafilter needs to be attached to the group head so that it heats up too. Similarly, the cups need to be placed on the cup-warming tray.

② Dosing, distribution, and tamping

Ⓐ Dosing and distribution involve taking freshly ground coffee from the grinder and placing it in the basket of the portafilter, which you have already wiped with a cloth, then leveling the coffee grounds, without compressing them, using one's fingers or a tool or by tapping the portafilter.
Ⓑ Very light leveling, delicately compacting at the same time.
  Firmer compacting exerting a pressure of around 33 lb, keeping one's arm as vertical as possible. Take care not to make any cracks in the grounds by pressing too hard!
Ⓒ Polishing the surface by rotating the tamper under its own weight.

USING A BARISTA-STYLE DOSING GRINDER

Baristas do not fill up the doser with ground coffee, as the coffee would then deteriorate. They use it as a single doser by running the grinder and actively shaking the lever to fill the portafilter.

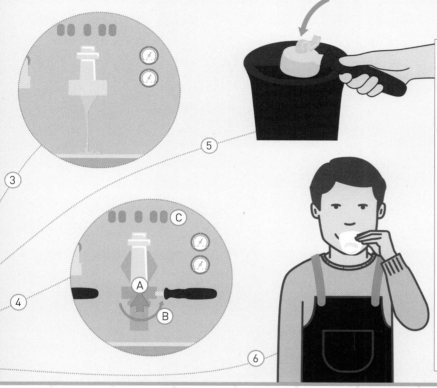

3

5

4

C

A

B

6

TAMPERS

The *tamper* is a tool the barista uses. Tampers are available in various materials with handles of different shapes and lengths for different requirements. The diameter of the base has to match that of the basket. Standard professional tampers have a diameter of 58 mm.

(3) **Purge**

Water is passed through the distribution screen (the "shower screen" in the group) for two or three seconds before locking the portafilter in place in order to stabilize the extraction temperature in machines with a heat exchanger, but above all to purge the shower screen of any particles of coffee left behind from the last extraction.

(4) **Extraction**

The extraction of the espresso must be initiated immediately once the handle is locked into the group to prevent the coffee grounds from cooking. It is also advisable to check beforehand that the gasket face and the lugs of the portafilter are clean.

(5) **Emptying**

The puck of coffee is emptied into the "knock box," a dump box provided for this purpose. Then all that remains is to wipe out the filter with a special cloth to get rid of any residue left behind.

(6) **Consumption**

The espresso is drunk right away. Now the day can begin!

THE STRENGTH OF THE ESPRESSO

Concentration, strength, intensity, extraction level: here's a guide to using the correct terminology and understanding what it refers to.

EXTRACTION   CONCENTRATION = STRENGTH

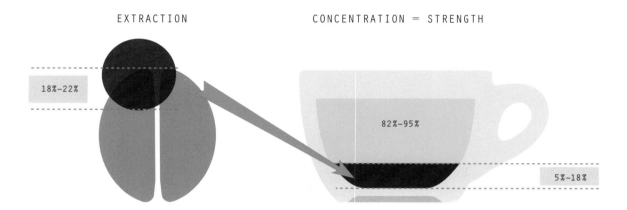

18%–22%

82%–95%

5%–18%

BREWING A COFFEE INVOLVES EXTRACTING 18–22 PERCENT BY MASS OF THE SOLUBLE COMPONENTS OF THE GROUND COFFEE.

THE EXTRACTED MATERIAL IS THEN DILUTED IN A CERTAIN AMOUNT OF WATER, SO THAT IT COMPRISES BETWEEN 5 AND 18 PERCENT OF THE FINAL BEVERAGE.

The degree of extraction determines the balance of the espresso.

There are two hazards to avoid:

UNDEREXTRACTION (LEVEL < 18%)
=
THE ESPRESSO HAS A FLAT, SOUR TASTE

OVEREXTRACTION (LEVEL > 22%)
=
BITTER OR EVEN ASTRINGENT COFFEE

The degree of concentration determines the strength, or taste intensity, of the espresso.

TDS OF BETWEEN 5 AND 8%
= A *LUNGO* (LONG),
IN OTHER WORDS, A VERY DILUTE ESPRESSO

TDS OF BETWEEN 8 AND 12%
= A CLASSIC/NORMAL OR REGULAR ESPRESSO

TDS OF BETWEEN 12 AND 18%
= A *RISTRETTO*,
IN OTHER WORDS, A VERY CONCENTRATED ESPRESSO

TDS

The concentration of solids in the final drink is known as TDS: total dissolved solids. It's an abbreviation you're sure to come across a lot if you start taking an interest in coffee from the technical side!

STYLES OF ESPRESSO

Espresso is not just espresso. It comes in many forms. Short, long … the way in which it is prepared differs by region, but also, first and foremost, according to individual taste.

THE SHORTER THE ESPRESSO, THE FULLER BODIED AND MORE POTENT IT IS.

Long black

If you prefer an espresso that is lighter than a *lungo* without the grounds being overextracted, the answer is the long black. This style of coffee originated in Australia and New Zealand. It is made by pulling an espresso into a cup prefilled with hot water. This makes the coffee more dilute, but it remains balanced and keeps its crema.

Americano

An Americano is an espresso lengthened with water after extraction.

The crema dissipates, making it lighter than a long black. It derives its name from the GIs based in Italy at the end of the Second World War, who made a habit of lengthening their espresso with hot water.

ESPRESSO BY THE NUMBERS

Brewing an espresso is one thing, but improving and fine-tuning it is quite another. It calls for both knowledge and experience, because there are a whole host of factors that come into play. "Calibration" is the term used to refer to all the adjustments made to the various parameters that contribute to a successful brew.

In theory

It was Achille Gaggia, the inventor of the lever espresso machine, who set the values of these parameters in 1947. Only the dose of ground coffee, initially set at 7 g per cup, has been revised up. The other values have remained unchanged for the last seventy years!

In practice

When setting the parameters for the extraction of the espresso on a traditional machine, you should always use the two-cup basket. When switching to a one-cup basket, all you need to do is divide the dose of ground coffee in half, as the volume per cup and the extraction time stay the same. But an espresso brewed with the one-cup portafilter will always be less flavorful because the group of the machine is designed for a two-cup basket.

THE FIVE PARAMETERS
THAT HAVE AN IMPACT ARE:

THE TEMPERATURE ④

THE EXTRACTION TIME,
THE GRIND SIZE ③

THE PRESSURE ⑤

THE DOSE OF GROUNDS ①

THE SHOT VOLUME ②

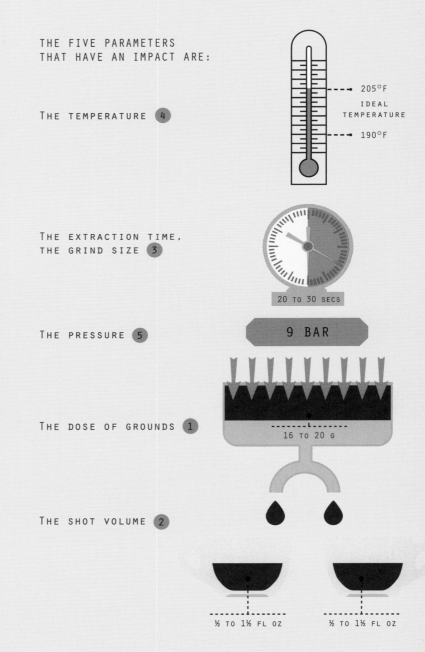

205°F
IDEAL TEMPERATURE
190°F

20 TO 30 SECS

9 BAR

16 TO 20 G

½ TO 1½ FL OZ   ½ TO 1½ FL OZ

8 TO 10 G

½ TO 1½ FL OZ

1 THE DOSE OF GROUND COFFEE

The dose of grounds affects the body and strength of flavor of the coffee. Reducing the dose makes the espresso blander. The standard weight specified by Achille Gaggia of 14 g for the two-cup basket has been revised up over the years to around 18 g, with a range of 16 g to 20 g, depending on the coffee bean (variety, terroir, roast level, freshness) and the desired shot volume.

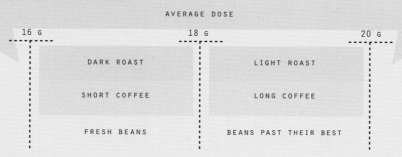

AVERAGE DOSE

16 G	18 G	20 G
DARK ROAST	LIGHT ROAST	
SHORT COFFEE	LONG COFFEE	
FRESH BEANS	BEANS PAST THEIR BEST	

ACCURATE TO A TENTH OF A GRAM!

Espresso is the most unforgiving coffee-brewing method. The dose of grounds needs to be accurate to a tenth of a gram! A coffee scoop (7 g) is not accurate enough because it does not take into account the fineness/coarseness of the grind, and not all coffees have the same density.

These frustrations can be avoided by using scales to weigh out the ground coffee. If you use a doserless grinder equipped with a timer, it is possible to program the dose of grounds produced, but you have to adjust the fineness first.

2 THE SHOT VOLUME

It is difficult to measure accurately the total volume of coffee because of the variation in the thickness of the crema. That is why volume is measured in terms of mass (1 g = about 1.5 ml with crema).

A LITTLE SET OF PRECISION SCALES ACCURATE TO 1/10 OF A GRAM IS PERFECT!

RATIO OF 1	RATIO OF 2	RATIO OF 3
RISTRETTO	ESPRESSO	*LUNGO*
18 G	18 G	18 G
9 G 9 G	18 G 18 G	27 G 27 G

FOR EACH STYLE OF ESPRESSO, THERE IS A RATIO BETWEEN THE MASS OF THE SHOT OF COFFEE AND THE INITIAL DOSE OF GROUNDS.

ESPRESSO BY THE NUMBERS

3 THE GRIND SIZE AND EXTRACTION TIME

To produce a balanced espresso, the coffee flow time has to be between twenty and thirty seconds. The count starts at the moment the extraction button is pressed, and the first droplets come out of the spouts on the portafilter five to ten seconds later.

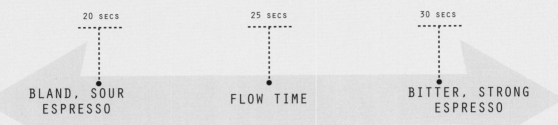

20 SECS — BLAND, SOUR ESPRESSO

25 SECS — FLOW TIME

30 SECS — BITTER, STRONG ESPRESSO

The flow rate depends on:

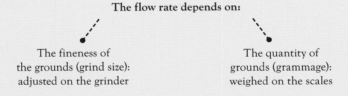

The fineness of the grounds (grind size): adjusted on the grinder

The quantity of grounds (grammage): weighed on the scales

Grind size problems and solutions:

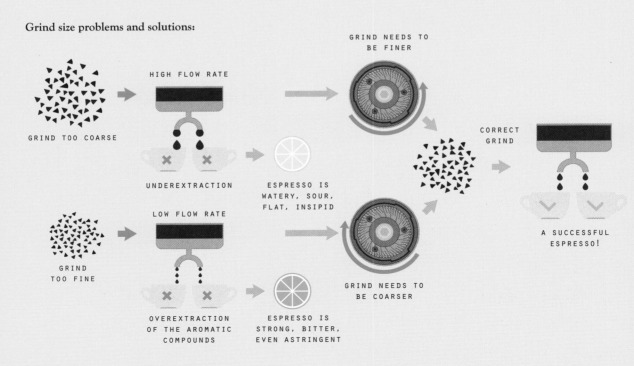

GRIND TOO COARSE

HIGH FLOW RATE

UNDEREXTRACTION

ESPRESSO IS WATERY, SOUR, FLAT, INSIPID

GRIND NEEDS TO BE FINER

GRIND TOO FINE

LOW FLOW RATE

OVEREXTRACTION OF THE AROMATIC COMPOUNDS

ESPRESSO IS STRONG, BITTER, EVEN ASTRINGENT

GRIND NEEDS TO BE COARSER

CORRECT GRIND

A SUCCESSFUL ESPRESSO!

4 TEMPERATURE

Adjusting the temperature enables you to influence the rate of extraction and the balance of sour/bitter flavors. The right temperature depends on several variables.

- **The roast level of the coffee beans:** A high temperature facilitates the extraction of the aromatic components and tempers the sourness of a lightly roasted bean; a medium temperature limits the bitterness of an overroasted bean.
- **The density of the bean:** A dense variety like bourbon will tolerate a high temperature better than a large bean like pacamara, which will burn more easily.
- **The dose of grounds:** The fall in the temperature of the extraction water is proportional to the grammage.
- **The length of the shot:** The risk of burning the grounds increases with the amount of water that passes through them.

TEMPERATURE STABILITY

An unstable machine means you are unable to serve several identical espressos in succession. This concern, much discussed in the 1990s, has attracted less attention in recent times, yet temperature remains a fundamental factor affecting the taste: even an amateur taster is able to tell the difference between two espressos pulled with a temperature differential of less than 2°F!

A COMBINATION OF TRIAL & ERROR AND EXPERIENCE WILL HELP YOU GET GOOD AT ANTICIPATING AND IMPROVING THE EXTRACTION TEMPERATURE.

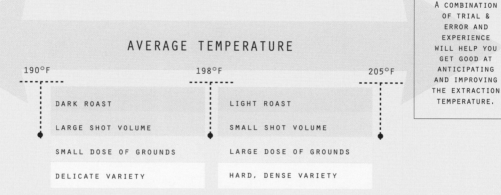

AVERAGE TEMPERATURE

190°F	198°F	205°F
DARK ROAST	LIGHT ROAST	
LARGE SHOT VOLUME	SMALL SHOT VOLUME	
SMALL DOSE OF GROUNDS	LARGE DOSE OF GROUNDS	
DELICATE VARIETY	HARD, DENSE VARIETY	

Barista tips

Good practices
- Unless otherwise indicated on the coffee bag, base your calculations on average values.
- Vary the parameters one at a time to allow you to properly assess the effect of each one.
- Note down the taste results following each adjustment. Ultimately it is the palate that will judge how well balanced the shot of coffee is!

Learn to read the coffee residue
The traces of caffeol left in the bottom of the basket after the puck of coffee has been emptied out are an indicator of the degree of extraction, which can be cross-checked with the other parameters and the result in the cup.

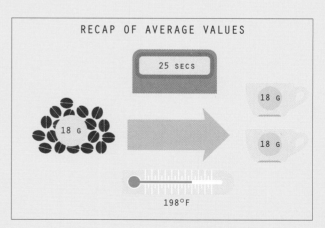

RECAP OF AVERAGE VALUES

25 SECS

18 G

18 G

18 G

198°F

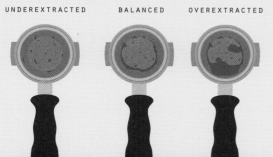

UNDEREXTRACTED   BALANCED   OVEREXTRACTED

As a last resort
If you find your coffee too sour even after adjusting the parameters, there is a trick that works equally well with all espresso machines (automatic, capsule, etc.): let the first drops that come out of the machine drip outside the cup. This has the effect of rebalancing the coffee flavors slightly.

ESPRESSO MAP

This map summarizes and sets out visually the effect of the various parameters on the extraction rate, the concentration, and the result in the cup.

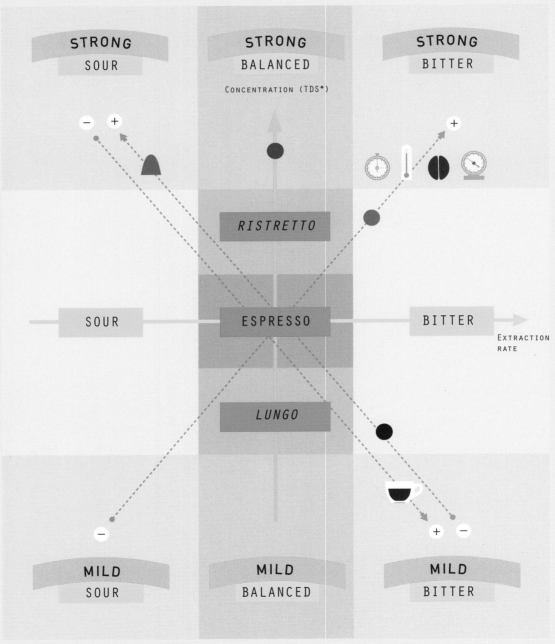

STRONG
SOUR

STRONG
BALANCED

Concentration (TDS*)

STRONG
BITTER

RISTRETTO

SOUR

ESPRESSO

BITTER

Extraction rate

LUNGO

MILD
SOUR

MILD
BALANCED

MILD
BITTER

*TDS: Total Dissolved Solids. See page 52.

How to read the map

- THE **HORIZONTAL AXIS** SHOWS THE DEGREE OF EXTRACTION, WHICH DETERMINES THE SOUR/BITTER BALANCE OF THE COFFEE.

- THE **VERTICAL AXIS** SHOWS THE DEGREE OF CONCENTRATION: FROM A MILD COFFEE TO A STRONG COFFEE.

- ON THE **DIAGONAL**, THE PARAMETERS:

  DOSE OF COFFEE GROUNDS

  SHOT VOLUME

  EXTRACTION TIME
  (GRIND SIZE)

  TEMPERATURE

  ROAST LEVEL

  EXTRACTION PRESSURE

Note that increasing the weight of the coffee grounds produces an increase in TDS, but reduces the degree of extraction. Conversely, lengthening the espresso, and therefore increasing the volume in the cup, makes the coffee milder (lower TDS), but also bitterer (higher degree of extraction). Increasing the other adjustable parameters (extraction time and temperature) brings the strength and bitterness of the coffee to the fore.

The balanced zones are located around the vertical axis. Depending on the desired concentration, the espresso's representative dot needs to be located within the *ristretto*, espresso, or *lungo* zone. If the espresso is not correctly calibrated, its representative dot will be located outside, in one of the eight peripheral zones representing specific symptoms. The barista can adjust the parameters in such a way as to bring the espresso's representative dot back within the balanced zone.

Examples

The examples are represented by the colored dots on the chart. Adjusting one of the parameters causes the dot to move along the axis of the parameter in question.

A COFFEE WHOSE PARAMETERS HAVE NOT BEEN PROPERLY MANAGED

Solution:
Reduce the extraction time to bring the coffee into the Espresso zone, and/or reduce the shot volume to bring the coffee into the *Ristretto* zone if you are after a tighter brew.

A DILUTE, BITTER COFFEE: FRENCH-STYLE!

Solution:
Reduce the shot volume (shorter coffee) and increase the dose of coffee grounds. This would move the blue dot into the Espresso zone in the center of the chart.

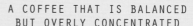

A COFFEE THAT IS BALANCED BUT OVERLY CONCENTRATED

The degree of extraction is correct.

Solution:
Increase the shot volume and reduce the flow time to counteract the mechanical increase in the degree of extraction. The dot will then move into the *Ristretto* zone or even the Espresso zone, depending on the size of the adjustment.

IT DOESN'T TASTE RIGHT! WHY?

"I've been trying for months now to produce a good espresso at home. I've tried everything. I've changed the machine, the coffee, the water. It makes no difference; my coffee is still nothing like the petit noir I got to enjoy when traveling in France . . . " Do you suffer the same frustration? A bad espresso is not the end of the world. It's possible to pinpoint what's causing the problem and, above all, figure out how to fix it.

It is hard for the uninitiated to find the right words to describe the shortcomings of a bad coffee, except to say with certainty that it is no good. A bad espresso may lack body, or may be overly bitter, sour, or pungent, offering little or nothing in the way of aromas, and a nonexistent finish.

Coffee is a product that does not tolerate mediocrity, particularly when it is brewed as an espresso. The process of bringing the ground coffee into contact with hot water under high pressure exerts harsh forces on the coffee and quickly brings out the qualities of the bean . . . but also its faults. Hence, every aspect of its preparation matters.

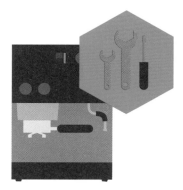

A machine that is underperforming, not properly looked after, maladjusted, or faulty

Although espresso machines have become a popular appliance to have at home, not all machines are equal, and it is essential to look after them properly. In particular, the internal components need to be kept free of coffee oil, and the pipework needs to be protected from limescale.

GO TO PAGE 46 FOR HOW TO LOOK AFTER YOUR MACHINE.

Cold or unsuitable cups

The impact of the drinking vessel is too often underestimated. As with wines or spirits, the shape, size, temperature, and material of the cup play important parts in how the flavors and fragrances of the coffee are perceived.

GO TO PAGE 30 TO CHOOSE YOUR CUP.

No coffee grinder

Unlike coffee beans, which maintain their qualities for several days once the package has been opened, ground coffee can lose its aromas in a matter of minutes, as the oxidation rate increases considerably due to the grounds being exposed to the air. Oxidized coffee will never make a good coffee. So it is vital to have a coffee grinder, and specifically a burr coffee grinder, alongside your espresso machine. It allows you to obtain fresh ground coffee, ground to the ideal fineness, perfect for brewing a *petit noir* just the way you like it.

GO TO PAGE 22 TO CHOOSE THE RIGHT GRINDER.

A grinder that is faulty or not properly looked after

The coffee beans regularly passing through the grinder leave behind oily deposits (caffeol) between the burrs and around the grind chamber. Over time, a rancid flavor may contaminate the fresh grounds, and the burrs will eventually wear out. So it is vital to clean your grinder as regularly as you do your espresso machine.

GO TO PAGE 25 FOR HOW TO LOOK AFTER YOUR GRINDER.

Extraction parameters not set correctly

The extraction of coffee under high pressure is a sophisticated process, the parameters of which must be correctly and accurately set. Indeed, the whole art of the barista consists of achieving the right calibration in order to produce the best possible espresso. Mastery of these parameters comes with experience, and a certain amount of trial and error.

GO TO PAGES 98–99 TO LEARN HOW TO BREW COFFEE BY NUMBERS.

Roasting issues

Roasting involves cooking the green coffee beans at high temperature. If the beans are not roasted for long enough, the espresso is liable to be flat and sour. Conversely, a bean that has been overroasted will produce a bitter coffee.

GO TO PAGE 106 TO FIND OUT ABOUT ROASTING AND ITS IMPLICATIONS.

Poor coffee beans

Coffee beans cultivated without due care in a terroir without character will never produce an exceptional coffee. A balanced drink is the best one can hope for. Opt for a good coffee. You can always ask for advice if need be.

GO TO PAGE 34 TO DISCOVER THE FINEST COFFEE BEANS.

Coffee that is not very fresh … or is too fresh !

Once roasted, the coffee bean retains its sensory qualities for several months in a sealed bag. After that it becomes rancid. A freshly roasted coffee is not ideal for consumption, either: the CO_2 that develops during roasting can cause extraction problems, with large bubbles visible in the flow. To obtain better results in the cup, you have to wait at least one week for the coffee beans to de-gas and lose their slightly metallic taste.

GO TO PAGE 116–117 TO FIND OUT HOW TO STORE YOUR COFFEE PROPERLY

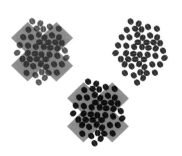

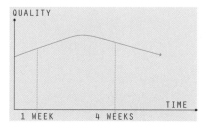

MILK, COFFEE & LATTE ART

The gentle combination of milk and coffee opens up all kinds of serving options designed to maximize both the taste experience and the visual appeal

Foaming the milk

When making milky drinks, the milk needs to be frothed up. It is simultaneously aerated, heated, and homogenized using the steam wand on the espresso machine. The resulting foam should display a dense, velvety texture, with bubbles so tiny that they are invisible to the naked eye.

WHOLE MILK OR UNPASTEURIZED MILK, 3.5% FAT. SKIMMED AND SEMI-SKIMMED MILK DO NOT PRODUCE A CREAMY ENOUGH FOAM.

STAINLESS STEEL PITCHERS FOR THEIR HEAT-CONDUCTING PROPERTIES:
• ONE 10 FL OZ PITCHER = 1 CAPPUCCINO
• ONE PINT PITCHER = 2 CAPPUCCINOS

The method

1

Fill the pitcher halfway, no matter what its size (up to about ½ inch below the spout).

2

Tilt the steam wand out at a slight angle from the vertical. Purge it.

3

Guide the steam wand into the spout of the pitcher. The nozzle should sit just below the surface of the milk, halfway between the center and the edge of the pitcher. Place one hand on the pitcher handle and the other underneath it to keep it in position and enable you to feel the rise in temperature.

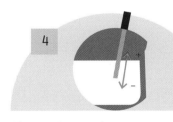

4

Phase 1: Turn on the steam to start incorporating air into the milk. Characteristic whistling sound. The milk increases in volume.
Phase 2: Position the steam wand slightly lower so the whistling stops. In this second phase, the emulsion is homogenized as a result of the whirling effect, and the milk is heated to 140–149°F. Take your hand away when the pitcher starts to feel burning hot.

5

Tap the pitcher on the counter to rid it of any bubbles, and finish with a broad swirl to "polish" the milk, giving it a silky surface sheen. It should have the texture of heavy cream.

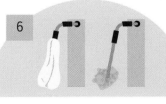

6

Wipe the steam wand with a cloth provided for that purpose and purge it to remove any milk residue.

TROUBLESHOOTING

Foam too thick? Too much air was incorporated in the first phase.
Foam that looks like hot milk? The initial whistling phase was not long enough.

The classic milk-pouring method

Incorporating the foamed milk into a ready-pulled espresso demands a particular technique: the milk has to flow under the coffee to make the coffee rise to the surface; the first flavor you should notice when you sip the drink is that of the coffee.

Hold the cup at an angle, then start pouring the milk 2 to 4 inches above the level of the coffee, aiming for the center. Provided it has been properly foamed, the milk should pass down through the coffee and not remain on the surface.

1

Once you have poured two-thirds of the milk, gradually set the cup upright and bring the pitcher down a lot lower, tilting it so as to deposit the milk on the surface.

2

3

4

Keep pouring in the foam until a white patch forms in the center. Set the pitcher upright to stop the flow of milk.

A good cappuccino has an unbroken ring of coffee, ensuring that the first flavor tasted on first sip is that of the coffee. If the disk of milk is too small, this means the lowering of the pitcher was started too late. And vice versa.

A GOOD FOAM

Test the volume of the foam with the back of a spoon: the foam must be at least ½ inch thick, and it should have a flexible, creamy texture.

THE HEART

This design is a cappuccino variant using the classic pour and is fairly simple to craft.

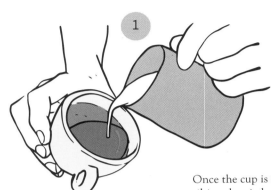

Start the pour as if you were doing a classic pour, adding a circular movement, then continue until the cup is full with a patch of white foam in the center.

Once the cup is full, perform a sideways movement by tilting the pitcher upward to extend the motif with a fine trickle of milk.

It is possible to add ripples to the heart. To do this, perform an alternating lateral movement as the disk of milk is forming.

THE TULIP

The tulip requires a little more skill, as the milk foam is poured in several stages.

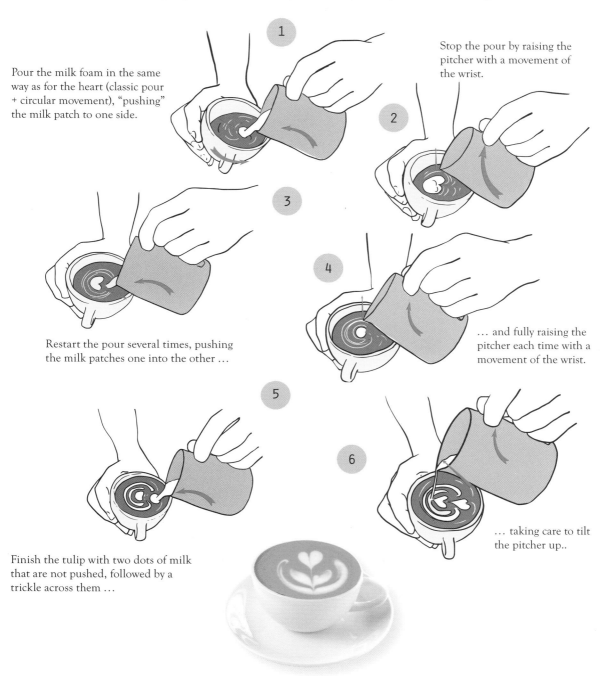

Pour the milk foam in the same way as for the heart (classic pour + circular movement), "pushing" the milk patch to one side.

Stop the pour by raising the pitcher with a movement of the wrist.

Restart the pour several times, pushing the milk patches one into the other …

… and fully raising the pitcher each time with a movement of the wrist.

Finish the tulip with two dots of milk that are not pushed, followed by a trickle across them …

… taking care to tilt the pitcher up..

THE ROSETTA

The rosetta is the hardest of the basic patterns to produce.
It needs perfectly foamed milk, dexterity … and several hours of practice!

Perform the pour in the same way as for the heart (classic pour + circular movement). As soon as a white patch appears, after lowering the pitcher, perform a broad lateral rocking movement while gradually raising the cup; the rosetta wave will form naturally.

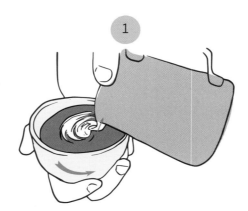

Continue the rocking movement, drawing the pitcher back to create the top of the rosetta.

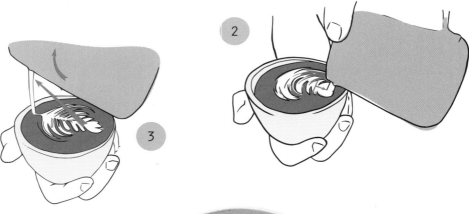

Pause briefly at the top to form a little heart, then take a line of milk across the pattern by tilting the pitcher up.

CAPPUCCINO & CO.

Cappuccino is the archetypal milky coffee-based drink. The cappuccino in the form we know today has its origins in Italy. It has a velvety texture, and the most complex coffee aromas are transformed into simpler, more accessible flavors (caramel, chocolate, etc.).

Its name is said to have derived from the color of the robes of the Capuchin monk Marco d'Aviano, who invented the cappuccino in the wake of the battle of Vienna in 1683.

1 Pull a shot of espresso (½ to 1½ fl oz) into a 5 to 6 fl oz cup.

2 Foam 5 fl oz of milk in a 10 fl oz pitcher.

3 Pour the foamed milk into the espresso.

WITH OR WITHOUT CHOCOLATE?

A cappuccino is traditionally prepared plain. But it is possible to decorate it with chocolate shavings or cocoa powder. If you create latte art on your cappuccino, sprinkle cocoa powder on the espresso before you pour in the milk foam.

Flat white

Originally from Australia and New Zealand, the flat white is a cappuccino with a finer milk foam. Traditionally prepared with two shots of espresso, it has a stronger coffee flavor.

6 FL OZ CUP

1 Pull two shots of espresso into about a 6 fl oz cup.

2 Foam 5 fl oz of milk in a 10 fl oz pitcher. Set the position of the nozzle so that you incorporate less air than for a cappuccino foam, giving you a denser, less fluffy texture.

3 Pour the foamed milk into the coffee.

Babyccino

The babyccino is a coffee-free drink, intended for children, consisting of milk and milk foam. It appeared on the scene in the 1990s in Australian and New Zealand coffee shops, where customers would come and bring their children.

7 FL OZ GLASS

1 Foam 5 fl oz of milk in a 10 fl oz pitcher (heating the milk less than for a cappuccino).

2 Pour the foamed milk into the cup or glass.

3 Sprinkle with cocoa powder.

Caffè latte

The **caffè latte** in Italy, or latte in the English-speaking world, is similar to the flat white but comes in a much larger cup.

7 TO 10 FL OZ CUP

1 Pull one or two shots of espresso into a 7 to 10 fl oz cup, depending on the desired strength of the coffee.

2 Foam 9 fl oz of milk in a 1 pint pitcher. Set the position of the nozzle so that you incorporate less air than for a cappuccino foam, so as to achieve a denser, less fluffy texture.

3 Pour the foamed milk into the coffee.

Latte macchiato

The **latte macchiato** is a variation on the caffè latte in which the espresso is poured into the milk foam. It is served in a large glass, which allows the drinker to appreciate the different layers of the drink.

12 FL OZ CUP

1 Foam 8 to 10 fl oz of milk in a 1 pint pitcher. Set the position of the nozzle so that you incorporate plenty of air to achieve a fluffy milk foam. Pour the foam into the glass.

2 Pull one shot of espresso into a small 3½ fl oz stainless steel or china pitcher.

3 Pour the espresso carefully into the glass: the different densities of the ingredients result in the formation of different layers.

Macchiato

The **macchiato**, which means "stained" or "spotted" in Italian, is an espresso topped with a layer of milk foam.

3 FL OZ GLASS

1 Pull one shot of espresso into about a 3 fl oz glass.

2 Foam up a small amount of milk in a small pitcher.

3 Place one or two coffee-spoonfuls of milk foam on the espresso.

Cortado

A **cortado**, from the Spanish *cortar*, meaning "to cut," is similar to a French *café noisette*. It is an espresso with a dash of hot milk. In its contemporary version, the milk is foamed, which makes it a kind of mini cappuccino with a higher concentration of coffee (about one-third espresso and two-thirds milk).

3 FL OZ GLASS

1 Pull one shot of espresso into about a 3 fl oz glass.

2 Foam up a small amount of milk in a 10 fl oz pitcher.

3 Pour the foamed milk into the espresso.

Affogato

A cross between a drink and a dessert, the **affogato** is a gourmet recipe that is simple to make and combines hot and cold.

7 FL OZ CUP

1 Place a scoop of vanilla ice cream in the bottom of a 7 fl oz glass.

2 Extract a double espresso directly onto the scoop of ice cream.

Café au lait

The equivalent of Proust's madeleine for many coffee enthusiasts, whose first experience of coffee in their youth came in the shape of this drink, the café au lait is to the French what the cappuccino is to the Italians. A classic.

18 FL OZ BOWL

1 Brew 7 fl oz of filter coffee, preferably using a French press.

2 Heat 7 fl oz of milk in a saucepan over a gentle heat, or alternatively using the steam wand on your espresso machine, to a temperature of approximately 149°F.

3 Pour the coffee and the milk into a bowl.

Irish Coffee

In an **Irish coffee**, the fruitiness and lightness of Irish whiskey marry beautifully with the coffee. The cream needs to be well chilled so that it cools the beverage down. Irish coffee is not mixed with anything: it should be consumed on its own.

7 FL OZ GLASS

1 Brew 3½ fl oz of filter coffee in a French press.

2 Dissolve two coffee-spoonfuls of brown sugar in 1½ fl oz of Irish whiskey heated in a double boiler (or a heatproof bowl set over a pan of simmering water).

3 Pour the coffee into the glass (warmed beforehand with hot water to prevent the glass from breaking due to thermal shock) and stir in the whiskey.

4 Whip heavy cream lightly. Carefully float it on the surface of the coffee using the back of a spoon.

Cappuccino frappé

This is a free interpretation of the cappuccino in an iced, whipped version.

7 FL OZ GLASS

1 Foam 5 fl oz of milk in a 10 fl oz pitcher and pour the foamed milk onto a shot of espresso (½ to 1½ fl oz).

2 Pour ½ oz of sugar syrup into a small 3½ fl oz stainless steel or china pitcher.

3 Pour the cappuccino and the sugar into a shaker filled with 3 oz of ice cubes. Then shake vigorously for 30 seconds.

4 Pour into a 7 fl oz glass, filtering out the ice cubes.

ELEGANT

LONG

AROMATIC

NO CREMA

DELICATE

ATMOSPHERIC
PRESSURE

FINE

1.5% COFFEE

98.5% WATER

MILD

7 FL OZ
OR MORE

DRUNK
SLOWLY

TAKES TIME
TO PREPARE

FILTER COFFEE

While there is only one way to produce a true espresso, there are several methods of brewing a filter coffee, which fall into two categories: immersion or filtration. These are also referred to as slow or gentle methods, as opposed to the ultra-fast, harsh method used to prepare espresso.

Immersion

The principle is to mix the ground coffee with hot water in a container, then leave them in contact for a certain amount of time (between one and four minutes, depending on the method used). They are then separated to produce a drinkable coffee. This method makes for easy, even extraction because the coffee particles infuse uniformly in the water, and does not require any particular skills.

Filtration

This method involves extracting the coffee from the grounds, which are held in a filter. The hot water wets and passes through the grounds, then through the filter. The liquid containing the aromatic compounds and the oils runs down, under the effect of gravity, into a container placed underneath, while the damp grounds remain in the filter. Contrary to the immersion method, where the coffee/water contact time is controlled, the brewing time by the filtration method depends on the speed with which the water is poured into the filter basket, and the fineness of the coffee grounds. To ensure an even extraction, it is important to see that the grounds are uniformly wetted throughout the process.

Key information for each method

4 MIN
BREWING TIME

FINENESS OF THE GROUNDS

14 G

QUANTITY OF COFFEE

× 1

NUMBER OF CUPS

7 FL
OZ

QUANTITY OF WATER

WHAT YOU NEED
TO MAKE FILTER COFFEE

*Whether you choose to brew your filter coffee by immersion or filtration,
you will always need coffee (ground), water (hot, usually), and a few utensils.
Now you just need to find your ideal coffee maker.*

A GRINDER
(SEE PAGES 22–23)

SCALES

As in cake making, scales are an indispensable tool when it comes to preparing a filter coffee. Measuring out the coffee with a spoon or the amount of water by volume is too imprecise (water changes its volume according to its temperature). Measuring the coffee dose and the quantity of water by weight is much more accurate. For this you need a set of scales accurate to a tenth of a gram, with a platform large enough accommodate the pitcher or the coffee pot when you are weighing out the quantity of water to be added to the coffee.

A TIMER

A SPATULA,
A STIRRER

WATER
(SEE PAGES 26–27)

Whatever coffee maker you are using, make sure you at least use fresh, filtered water.

A KETTLE

FILTERS
(SEE PAGES 78–79)

Made of paper, cloth, or metal.
Round or corrugated. For siphon or V60.

A CUP, A MUG,
A GLASS
(SEE PAGES 30–31)

A must: a gooseneck kettle

You won't be able to properly prepare a coffee by the filtration method unless you have a special kettle with a gooseneck pouring spout. This gives you much better control of the flow of water than a traditional kettle, making for uniform extraction. There are some very good kettles available from Hario and Bonavita, which even offer one featuring a temperature regulator accurate to 1 degree.

A flow restrictor

To control the pour even more precisely and keep it even more constant, you can add a flow restrictor, an accessory that is particularly useful when you are brewing with a Hario V60 and is readily available on the Internet.

The ideal coffeemaker

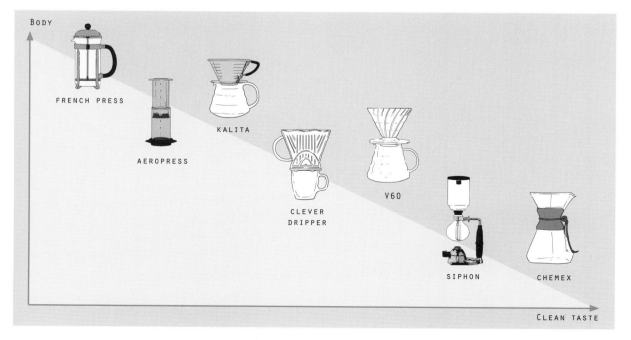

BODY

FRENCH PRESS

AEROPRESS

KALITA

CLEVER DRIPPER

V60

SIPHON

CHEMEX

CLEAN TASTE

FILTER COFFEE: THE TASTING EXPERIENCE

Filter coffee, just like espresso, can be tasted and evaluated according to clearly defined criteria. Long regarded as an inferior option, filter coffee is today enjoying a well-deserved resurgence.

The ritual

Filter coffee is much more accessible than espresso, both in financial and technical terms. However, there are certain rules that need to be followed to make a really good filter coffee and get the most out of it.

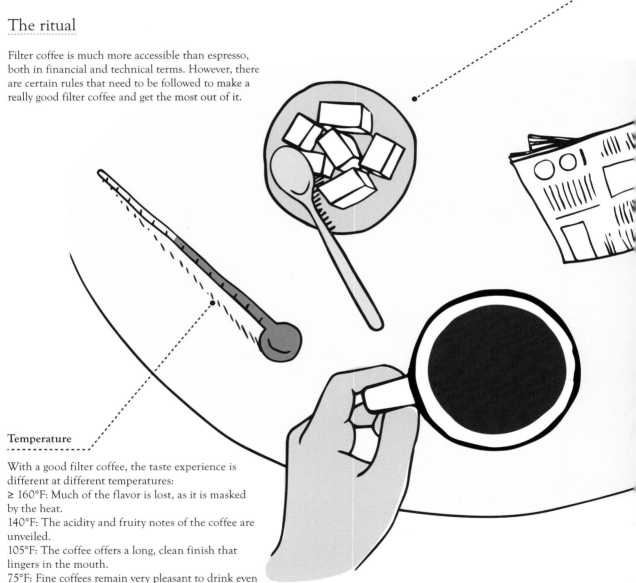

Temperature

With a good filter coffee, the taste experience is different at different temperatures:
≥ 160°F: Much of the flavor is lost, as it is masked by the heat.
140°F: The acidity and fruity notes of the coffee are unveiled.
105°F: The coffee offers a long, clean finish that lingers in the mouth.
75°F: Fine coffees remain very pleasant to drink even when cold.

A well-prepared filter coffee does not need sugar, which would inevitably mask its subtle taste and delicate notes. By contrast, a bad filter coffee, poorly brewed, that has a bitter taste and lacks mellowness and flavor, may be favorably rebalanced with the addition of sugar.

Sensations

The color of the coffee

The quality of the drinking vessel from which you drink your filter coffee has less of an impact on how it tastes than in the case of an espresso. A glass or a transparent mug allows you to appreciate the color of the filter coffee, and hence the roast level of the coffee beans:
• Dark-roasted beans produce a dark-colored, deep brown to black filter coffee.
• Light-roasted beans produce a light brown to red brew.

The nose

The fragrance that emanates from the filter coffee must be pleasant, with fruity, floral, or nutty notes. Any other note would tend to be deemed a negative attribute.

The taste

Of the five primary tastes, the most important for filter coffee is probably sourness, as it lends the coffee vibrancy and freshness, is associated with positive fruity notes, and gives depth to the coffee. However, this acidity must be of the right type (quinic acid is associated with astringency, acetic acid gives a tart flavor, etc.—see page 27) and not overly intense; otherwise unpleasant sensations could be transmitted.

The aromas

The aromatic range of a filter coffee is broader than that of an espresso. The aromas can be grouped into a number of categories: floral, fruity, grassy, nutty, caramelized, chocolaty, medicinal, spicy, and smoky.

As with an espresso, the aromas of a filter coffee (perceived by retronasal olfaction) supplement the fragrance (perceived by the nose), but these aromas are not necessarily identical to those of an espresso (see pages 36–39).

The body

Since a filter coffee is ten times less concentrated than an espresso, the notion of body is not judged on the same scale. The elements that contribute to its body are the components not dissolved by the water, which remain in suspension in the drink (sediments and oils), giving it thickness. Body is first and foremost a tactile feeling in the mouth that can be described as creamy, heavy, thick, light, weak, or watery. Whether the body is weak or highly intense, this feeling must be pleasant and enjoyable.

The flavor

Obviously, a filter coffee does not offer the same strength, or as much body, viscosity, and concentration as an espresso. Instead it is appreciated for its fineness, its delicacy, its length on the palate, its pleasant sourness, its silky body, and the transparency of its flavors. The tasting of a filter coffee can be likened to a long, relaxing journey that transports you into expansive landscapes alive with detail.

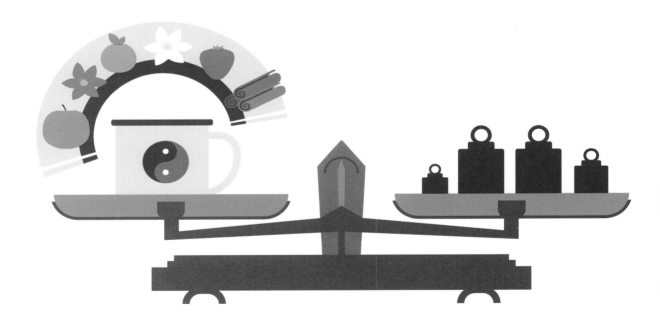

WHAT IS A COMPLEX COFFEE?

A complex coffee is one that, on tasting, offers a rich array of positive flavors (floral, fruity, spicy, etc.) at different temperatures, and a balanced and varied sensory experience (it may be well-rounded, tangy with some sweetness, etc.).

EXAMPLE OF A TASTING FORM

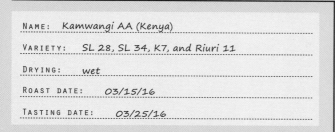

NAME: Kamwangi AA (Kenya)

VARIETY: SL 28, SL 34, K7, and Riuri 11

DRYING: wet

ROAST DATE: 03/15/16

TASTING DATE: 03/25/16

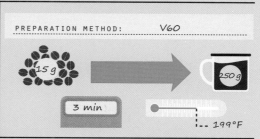

PREPARATION METHOD: V60

15 g → 250 g

3 min   199°F

NOSE

POSITIVES

✓ NUTS	TROPICAL FRUIT
RED FRUIT	CITRUS
STONE FRUIT	✓ FLORAL
VEGETAL	SPICY

NEGATIVES

TOBACCO	VEGETAL
BURNT	WOODY

NOTES: honey, jam

AROMAS

POSITIVES

✓ NUTS	TROPICAL FRUIT
✓ RED FRUIT	CITRUS
STONE FRUIT	FLORAL
VEGETAL	SPICY

NEGATIVES

TOBACCO	VEGETAL
BURNT	WOODY

NOTES: black currant, gooseberry, marzipan

ACIDITY

1   2   3   4 ✗   5

SWEETNESS

1   2 ✗   3   4   5

INTENSITY

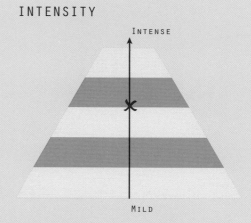

INTENSE

MILD

BODY

1   2   ✗ 3   4   5

BALANCE

1   2   3 ✗   4   5

CLEAN CUP

1   2   3   4 ✗   5

LENGTH OF FINISH

1   2   ✗ 3   4   5

FLAVOR, GENERAL SENSATION

Sweet nose, with an elegant, mellow
acidity. Medium-bodied, up-front
aromas and clean cup. A lovely
Kenyan coffee.

COFFEE FILTERS

Preparing filter coffee involves bringing ground coffee into contact with hot water.
The liquid containing the extracted material percolates through and is separated
from the grounds by means of a filter.

Paper filter

The paper filter, invented by Melitta in 1908, is the filter most widely used today. It is inexpensive and comes either bleached or unbleached. The former is preferable, because an unbleached filter has a more noticeable paper taste.

Cloth filter

The cloth filter (usually made of cotton), forerunner of the paper filter, gives a clean cup with more texture than a paper filter.

THE

It retains all the insoluble elements as well as most of the coffee oils, giving the cleanest cup of all filter coffees, with the greatest flavor clarity. It is also the easiest to find in stores.

THE

It is reusable, and retains a large proportion of the insoluble elements while allowing some of the coffee oil to seep through; the coffee obtained in this way is both rich and aromatic.

THE

It can only be used once and needs to be rinsed with water beforehand, otherwise it will transmit an unpleasant paper taste to the coffee.

THE

A cloth filter needs cleaning after each use and has to be stored wet in a sealed container in the refrigerator. If not, the fabric will give off bad smells that will contaminate the coffee during brewing.

Metal filter

Metal filters are not just reserved for espresso machines: they are used in some cases for brewing filter coffee as well. The metal filter contains masses of holes of a predefined diameter that let liquid through, but also sediment, insoluble elements, and coffee oils.

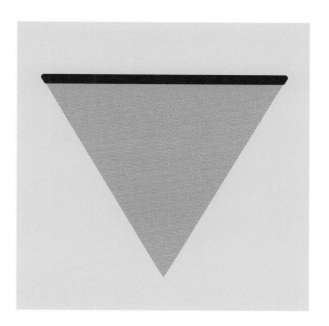

THE **+** Easy to clean, reusable, and has no particular storage requirements. The coffee filtered by this method has more texture, more body, and is also more opaque.

THE **−** Flavor clarity is not as good as with other types of filter.

The right filter for the coffee maker

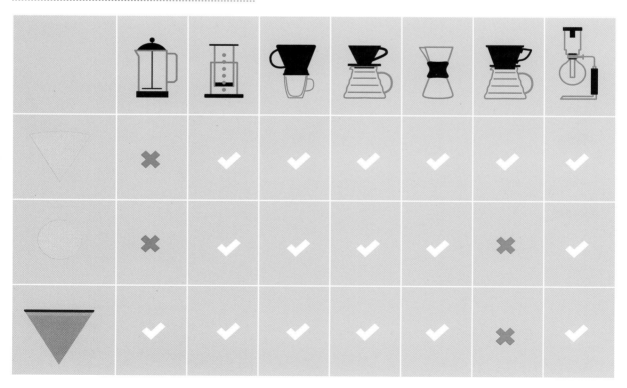

	✗	✓	✓	✓	✓	✓	✓
	✗	✓	✓	✓	✓	✗	✓
	✓	✓	✓	✓	✓	✗	✓

THE FRENCH PRESS

The French press, known as the cafetière in France, is the easiest type of coffee maker to use.

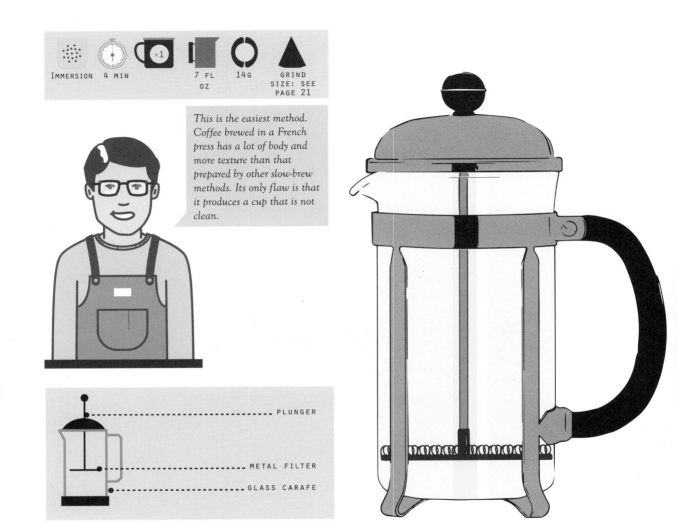

IMMERSION   4 MIN   7 FL   14G   GRIND
                            OZ   SIZE: SEE
                                           PAGE 21

×1

This is the easiest method. Coffee brewed in a French press has a lot of body and more texture than that prepared by other slow-brew methods. Its only flaw is that it produces a cup that is not clean.

PLUNGER

METAL FILTER

GLASS CARAFE

FILTERING COFFEE BREWED IN A FRENCH PRESS

Coffee brewed in a French press contains a great many particles in suspension. For a coffee with less sediment, you can filter it using a coffee filter; you will be able to see all the insoluble particles you have removed by doing this. The resulting coffee has less body, but flavor perception is improved.

Method

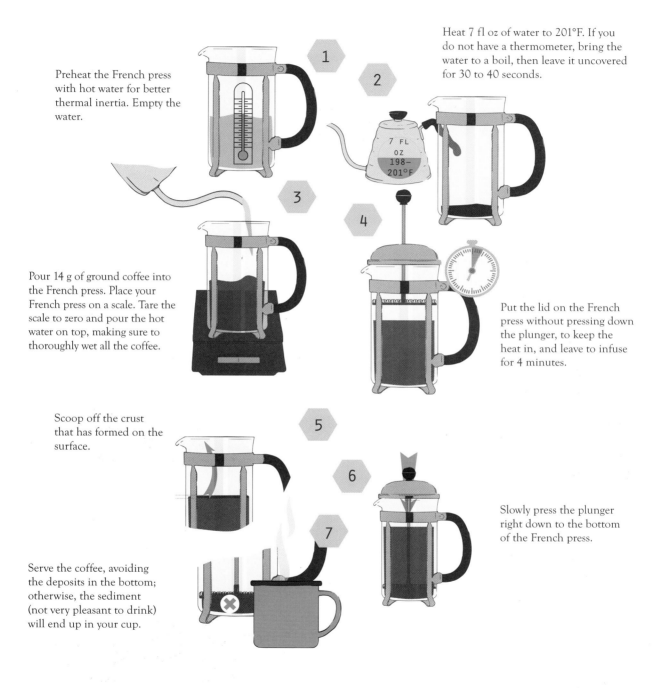

Preheat the French press with hot water for better thermal inertia. Empty the water.

1

2 Heat 7 fl oz of water to 201°F. If you do not have a thermometer, bring the water to a boil, then leave it uncovered for 30 to 40 seconds.

3 Pour 14 g of ground coffee into the French press. Place your French press on a scale. Tare the scale to zero and pour the hot water on top, making sure to thoroughly wet all the coffee.

4 Put the lid on the French press without pressing down the plunger, to keep the heat in, and leave to infuse for 4 minutes.

5 Scoop off the crust that has formed on the surface.

6 Slowly press the plunger right down to the bottom of the French press.

7 Serve the coffee, avoiding the deposits in the bottom; otherwise, the sediment (not very pleasant to drink) will end up in your cup.

THE AEROPRESS

Invented in 2005 by Alan Adler, the founder of Aerobie, Inc., the Aeropress is a plastic coffee maker that is very easy to use.

| IMMERSION | 1 MIN 30 SECS | PAPER | ×1 | 7 FL OZ | 14G | GRIND SIZE: SEE PAGE 21 |

Brewing is quicker than with a French press. And thanks to the paper filter, there is less sediment left in the cup.

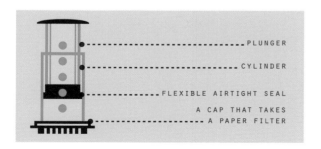

PLUNGER

CYLINDER

FLEXIBLE AIRTIGHT SEAL

A CAP THAT TAKES
A PAPER FILTER

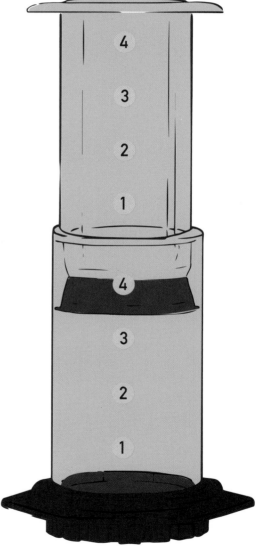

Methods

Heat 9 fl oz of water to 198–201°F. If you do not have a thermometer, bring the water to a boil and leave it uncovered for 30 to 45 seconds.

Place a filter in the cap and rinse with a little water.

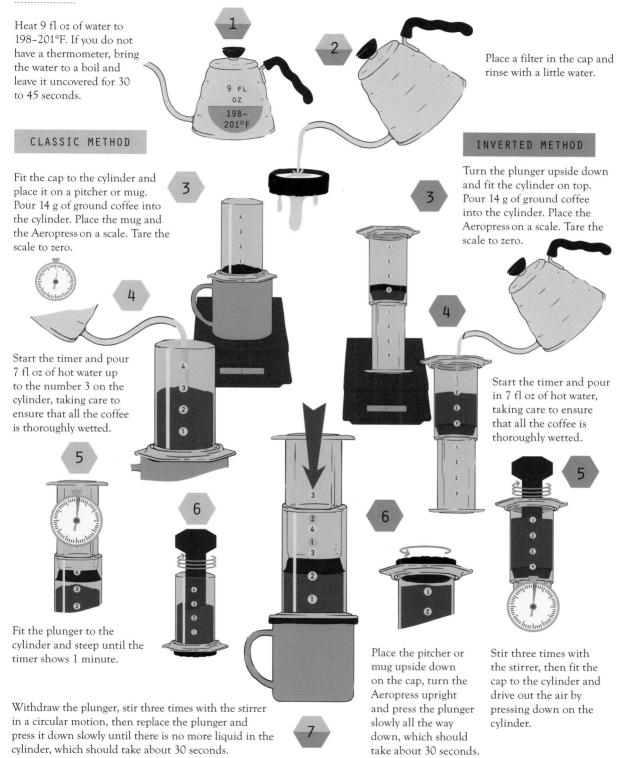

CLASSIC METHOD

Fit the cap to the cylinder and place it on a pitcher or mug. Pour 14 g of ground coffee into the cylinder. Place the mug and the Aeropress on a scale. Tare the scale to zero.

Start the timer and pour 7 fl oz of hot water up to the number 3 on the cylinder, taking care to ensure that all the coffee is thoroughly wetted.

Fit the plunger to the cylinder and steep until the timer shows 1 minute.

Withdraw the plunger, stir three times with the stirrer in a circular motion, then replace the plunger and press it down slowly until there is no more liquid in the cylinder, which should take about 30 seconds.

INVERTED METHOD

Turn the plunger upside down and fit the cylinder on top. Pour 14 g of ground coffee into the cylinder. Place the Aeropress on a scale. Tare the scale to zero.

Start the timer and pour in 7 fl oz of hot water, taking care to ensure that all the coffee is thoroughly wetted.

Stir three times with the stirrer, then fit the cap to the cylinder and drive out the air by pressing down on the cylinder.

Place the pitcher or mug upside down on the cap, turn the Aeropress upright and press the plunger slowly all the way down, which should take about 30 seconds.

THE CLEVER COFFEE DRIPPER

This coffee maker, designed by the Taiwanese company ABID (Absolutely Best Idea Development),
combines the immersion and filtration methods,
but the extraction itself is primarily by immersion.

| IMMERSION + FILTRATION | 3 MIN 30 SECS | PAPER | 10 FL OZ | 14G | GRIND SIZE: SEE PAGE 21 |

Of all the immersion methods, this is the one that leaves the least amount of sediment in the cup.

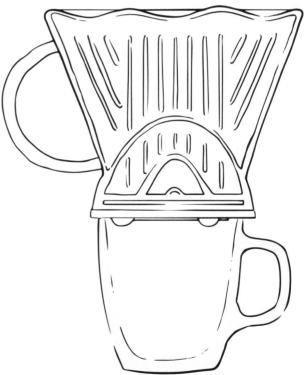

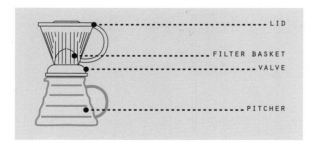

- LID
- FILTER BASKET
- VALVE
- PITCHER

Method

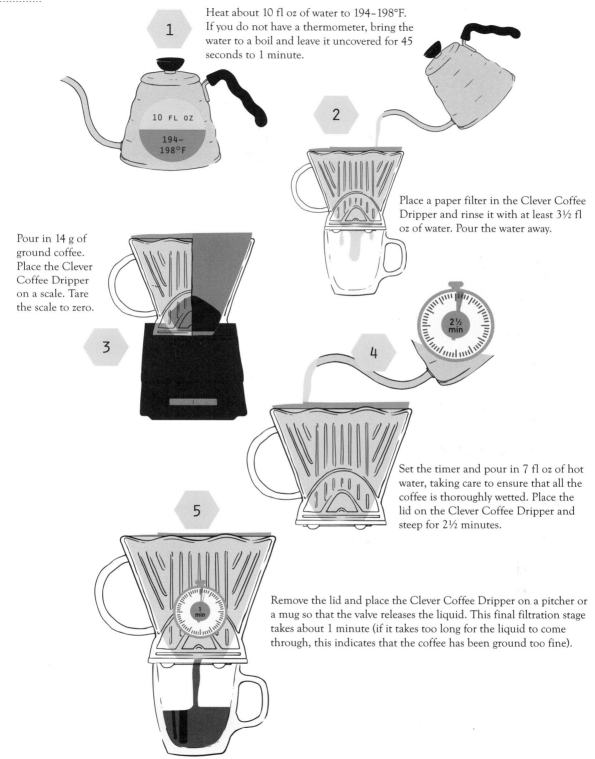

1 Heat about 10 fl oz of water to 194–198°F. If you do not have a thermometer, bring the water to a boil and leave it uncovered for 45 seconds to 1 minute.

10 FL OZ
194–198°F

2 Place a paper filter in the Clever Coffee Dripper and rinse it with at least 3½ fl oz of water. Pour the water away.

3 Pour in 14 g of ground coffee. Place the Clever Coffee Dripper on a scale. Tare the scale to zero.

2 ½ min

4 Set the timer and pour in 7 fl oz of hot water, taking care to ensure that all the coffee is thoroughly wetted. Place the lid on the Clever Coffee Dripper and steep for 2½ minutes.

1 min

5 Remove the lid and place the Clever Coffee Dripper on a pitcher or a mug so that the valve releases the liquid. This final filtration stage takes about 1 minute (if it takes too long for the liquid to come through, this indicates that the coffee has been ground too fine).

THE SIPHON

Invented in the 1830s, this appliance is also known as a "vacpot."
It is quite an impressive-looking contraption, and the method is equally spectacular.

IMMERSION + FILTRATION | 1 MIN 50 SECS | CLOTH | ×1 | 10 FL OZ | 16G | GRIND SIZE: SEE PAGE 21

This produces a very delicate cup of coffee that is very clean, with excellent flavor clarity.

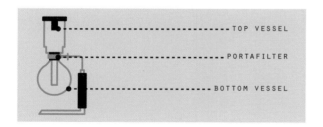

TOP VESSEL

PORTAFILTER

BOTTOM VESSEL

HAVE YOU JUST BOUGHT A SIPHON? READ ON!

The Hario siphon is supplied with an alcohol burner. This gives you no control at all over the heat, which is why it is advisable to acquire a gas burner, which enables you to finely control the heat and keep it constant

Method

Heat 10 fl oz of water to 194–198°F: if you do not have a thermometer, bring the water to a boil, then leave it uncovered for 45 seconds.

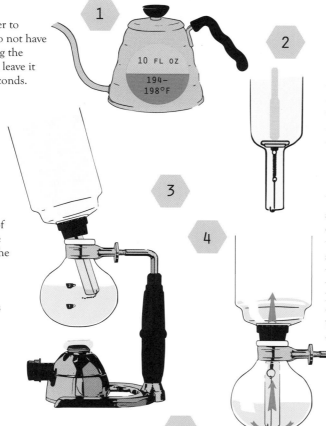

Rinse the filter. Insert the portafilter into the upper chamber of the siphon and fix it to the tube using the spring. Insert the filter and use the stirrer to get it properly centered.

Pour hot water into the lower chamber of the siphon up to the 2 cup mark. Insert the upper chamber into the lower chamber without sealing the system. Light the gas burner and place it under the lower chamber.

Bring the water to the boil, then seal the system by locking the upper chamber into the lower chamber—under the effect of the heat, the air will push the water through the tube, causing it to rise into the upper chamber. When the water has finished migrating into the upper chamber, adjust the heat to bring the water to 194–198°F (use a thermometer to check).

Pour in 16 g of ground coffee. Start the timer. Stir well with the stirrer to ensure the grounds are thoroughly wetted. Steep for 1 minute.

Switch off the gas burner and remove it—a vacuum will form, and the liquid will be drawn down by gravity and suction through the tube into the lower chamber. The filter separates the grounds from the extracted coffee. This final filtration stage takes 30 to 40 seconds. If it takes too long for the liquid to come through, this indicates that the coffee has been ground too fine.

THE HARIO V60

*Sold by the Japanese company Hario, the V60 is a coffee dripper in the shape of a V
(at an angle of 60 degrees, hence its name).*

| FILTRATION | 2 MIN 30 SECS TO 3 MIN | V60 FILTER | ×1 | | 10 FL OZ | 12-13G | GRIND SIZE: SEE PAGE 21 |

This method offers a neat compromise between body and flavor clarity

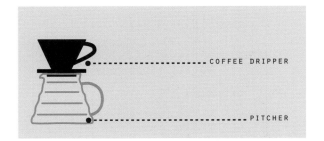

COFFEE DRIPPER

PITCHER

Method

Heat approximately 10 fl oz of water to 201°F. If you do not have a thermometer, bring the water to a boil and leave it uncovered for 30 to 40 seconds.

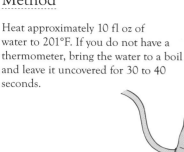

Pour in 12–13 g of coffee. Place the Hario and the pitcher on a scale. Tare the scale to zero.

Place a filter in the V60 and rinse well with at least 3½ fl oz of water to prevent any taste of paper transferring to the final brew. Discard the water

Start the timer and begin by pouring in 25 g of hot water, making sure all the coffee is moistened. Stir it to make sure it is evenly wetted.

After 30 seconds—the time it takes for the ground coffee to be saturated with water and start to bloom—pour in another 25 g of water, pouring clockwise in a circular motion, avoiding wetting the filter paper. Keep pouring in 25 g of water every 15 seconds until the scale shows 200 g. The total extraction time is generally between 2½ and 3 minutes. If the water trickles through too fast, the coffee has probably been ground too coarse. If it takes too long, it means the grind size is too fine.

THE CHEMEX

The Chemex, invented in 1941 by Dr. Peter Schlumbohm, is a complete coffee maker in the shape of an hourglass. The upper part is a portafilter and the lower part is a collecting vessel.

| FILTRATION | 3 MIN 30 SECS TO 4 MIN | CHEMEX FILTER | ×6 | 1¾ PINTS | 30–35G | GRIND SIZE: SEE PAGE 21 |

The coffee brewed with the Chemex does not have much body, but it is very fine, with excellent clarity of flavor.

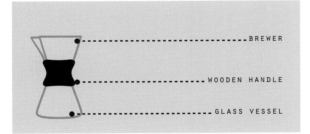

- - - - - - BREWER
- - - - - - WOODEN HANDLE
- - - - - - GLASS VESSEL

FOLDING THE CHEMEX FILTER

The paper filter for the Chemex is thicker than other paper filters and needs to be folded asymmetrically so that you end up with one layer of filter paper on one side of the brewer and three layers on the other side. For an alternative fold method, follow the steps shown opposite.

Method

Heat 1¾ pints of water to 201°F. If you do not have a thermometer, bring the water to a boil, then leave it uncovered for 30 to 40 seconds.

1¾ PT

201°F

Fold a filter, place it in the Chemex, and rinse well with at least 18 fl oz of water to rule out the possibility of any paper taste transferring to the final brew. Take out the filter. Empty out the water from the Chemex, then replace the filter.

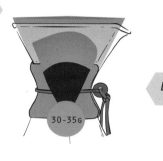

Pour in 30 to 35 g of coffee. Place the Chemex on a scale. Tare the scale to zero.

30-35G

Set the timer. Start by pouring in 100 g of water, taking care to wet all the grounds. Wait for 45 seconds—the time it takes for the grounds to be thoroughly saturated with water and start to bloom.

Pour in another 100 g of water in a clockwise circular motion, going from the center toward the edges and from the edges toward the center as if you were drawing a spiral.

The total extraction time is generally between 3½ and 4 minutes. If the water trickles through faster than that, the coffee has probably been ground too coarse. If it takes too long, it means the grind size is too fine.

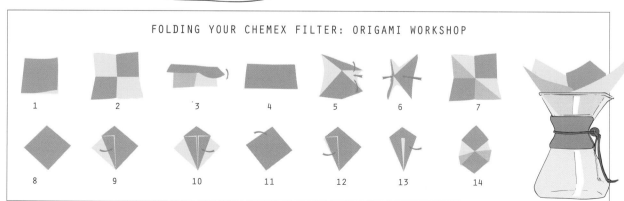

FOLDING YOUR CHEMEX FILTER: ORIGAMI WORKSHOP

1 2 3 4 5 6 7

8 9 10 11 12 13 14

THE KALITA WAVE

The Kalita Wave, a Japanese product, is a flat-bottomed coffee dripper
with three small holes in the bottom. It is used with a special scalloped filter.

FILTRATION | 3 MIN | KALITA FILTER | ×1 | 14 FL OZ | 18G | GRIND SIZE: SEE PAGE 21

*The coffee produced with
this coffee maker is full-bodied,
with well-developed flavors.*

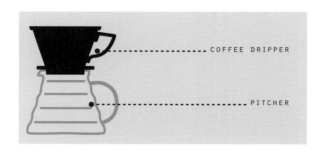

COFFEE DRIPPER

PITCHER

Method

1

Heat about 14 fl oz of water to 201°F. If you do not have a thermometer, bring the water to a boil and leave it uncovered for 30 to 40 seconds.

2

Place a filter in the Kalita Wave. Pour some hot water into the center of the filter so that it settles into position in the dripper. Discard the water. Unlike in the case of the V60 and the Chemex, the filter does not need to be rinsed with plenty of water to get rid of the taste of paper.

Pour in 18 g of coffee. Place the dripper and the pitcher on a scale. Tare the scale to zero.

3

4

Start the timer. Pour in 50 g of water, taking care to ensure that all the grounds are wetted. Wait 40 to 45 seconds to allow the grounds to become thoroughly saturated with water and to bloom (releasing CO_2), then pour in a further 50 g of water in a clockwise circular motion, moving from the center toward the edge, then from the edge toward the center, as if you were drawing a spiral. Avoid pouring water onto the filter paper. Pour in another 50 g of water before the water level reaches the top of the grounds. Repeat until the scales show 300 g. The total extraction time is about 3 minutes. If the water trickles through faster than that, that is a sure sign that the coffee has been ground too coarse. If it takes too long, it means the grind size is too fine.

THE MOKA POT

This coffee maker was inspired by Louis Bernard Rabaut's "washing machine" coffee maker invented in 1820. Patented in 1933 by Alfonso Bialetti, the moka pot is also known as the "Italian coffee maker." Bialetti still manufactures these coffee makers, which remain as popular as ever. Originally made of aluminum, the moka pot is now made of stainless steel and comes in various designs and sizes.

FILTRATION | 1 MIN | ×3 | 5 FL OZ | 15G | GRIND SIZE: SEE PAGE 21

This coffee maker produces a strong, relatively concentrated coffee (high coffee-to-water ratio) slightly resembling an espresso—although the pressure in a moka pot is around 1.5 bar at most, whereas an espresso machine operates at a pressure of the order of 8 to 10 bar. On account of its design and the very high temperature the water is heated to, the moka pot has a tendency to extract the bitter components of the coffee unless a few precautions are taken.

- LID
- SPOUT
- FILTER BASKET
- WATER RESERVOIR

Method

Put 15 g of coffee in the filter basket. Tap the edge to spread the grounds uniformly in the filter basket. Do not tamp.

Heat the water to 176°F in an electric kettle—this saves time and prevents the grounds from burning. Then fill the reservoir with hot water up to just below the valve (about 5 fl oz).

Screw on the top chamber. Place the coffee maker on the stovetop over low heat—leave the lid open so you can see how the extraction is progressing

As soon as the coffee starts to flow, lower the heat and time 1 minute before removing the moka pot from the heat. Do not wait for all the water to come through. If the coffee comes through in less than 1 minute, the grind is too coarse. If the coffee takes longer than 1 minute to come through, it means the grind is too fine.

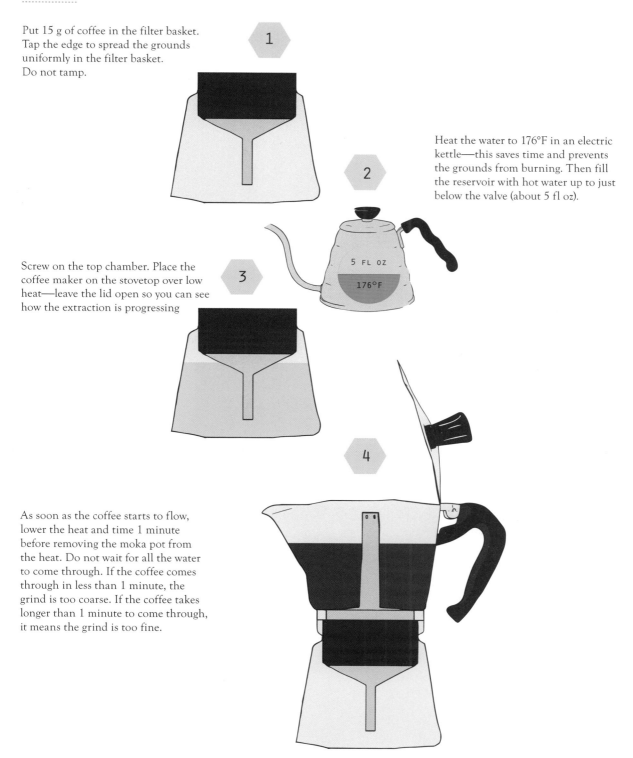

THE ELECTRIC COFFEE MAKER

The electric coffee maker was invented in the 1950s,
but it was only in the 1970s that it really caught on and became popular.

FILTRATION   5–6 MIN   PAPER   6–8   1¾ PINTS   60–70G   GRIND SIZE: SEE PAGE 21

Gives a balanced cup in which the acidity is less pronounced than with a manual V60. This coffee can also be said to be less developed, with less flavor complexity (the flavors are not so clear-cut).

SHOWER SCREEN

FILTER BASKET

CARAFE

HOT PLATE

THAT'S GRAVITY!

The cold water from the reservoir is drawn by gravity toward a chamber where an electric element heats the water to more than 194°F. The hot water passes through a tube to a shower screen, from which it drizzles slowly down onto the ground coffee sitting in a paper filter below. The coffee extracted by gravity trickles into a carafe placed beneath the filter basket, which sits on a hot plate to keep the brewed coffee warm as the rest filters through.

Method

1

Rinse the filter well with at least 7 fl oz of hot water to prevent the taste of paper from being transferred to the coffee—alternatively, you can pour the water into the reservoir and run the coffee machine without coffee. Tip the ground coffee into the filter.

2

Pour the water into the reservoir.

3

Set the time you want brewing to start, or start the machine if you would like to make coffee right now.

4

Once the coffee is brewed, do not keep it warm in the carafe for too long; either drink it or transfer it to a thermos flask, and do not keep it for any longer than 20 to 30 minutes. Any longer than that and the coffee will oxidize and deteriorate.

FILTER COFFEE
BY THE NUMBERS

Whatever method you are using, if you want to brew a good filter coffee, there are certain parameters you need to keep tabs on. Besides that, a little experience and a sense of curiosity are all you need ...

The grind

The finer the grind, the greater the surface area, and hence the greater the solubility on contact with water.

To craft a good filter coffee, the grind has to be coarser than for espresso, and above all as uniformly ground as possible: fine coffee particles tend to be overextracted on contact with hot water, producing a bitterness in the mouth and interfering with one's perception of the flavors. The fineness of the grind must be adjusted according to the method used, the quantity of coffee (and therefore water), and the type of filter in question.

The water temperature

Most of the components of the coffee are more soluble at high temperature. The optimum temperature is between 198–203°F.

Adjusting the temperature
Boiling water will burn the coffee, whereas if the water is not hot enough, the flavor potential of the coffee will not be fully unlocked.

The temperature also needs to be adjusted according to the roast level of the beans.

Dark roast: lower temperature (198°F or even lower)
Light roast: higher temperature (201–203°F).

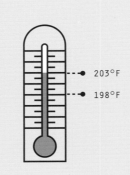

203°F
198°F

Adjusting the grind

IMMERSION METHOD

Issue	Explanation	Solution
The coffee is bitter, astringent, and dry, with an unpleasant aftertaste.	The coffee is overextracted.	Coarser grind
The coffee is overly sour and salty.	The coffee is under-extracted.	Finer grind

FILTRATION METHOD

Issue	Explanation	Solution
The coffee is bitter, astringent, and dry, with an unpleasant aftertaste.	The coffee is overextracted.	Coarser grind, then the coffee will percolate more quickly
The coffee is overly sour and flows through too quickly.	The coffee is under-extracted.	Finer grind, then the coffee will percolate more slowly

The coffee/water ratio

Filter coffee is ten times less concentrated than espresso. Compared to the latter, a filter coffee needs a smaller dose of coffee, but a larger quantity of water. Generally this ratio is 55–80 g of coffee per 1 liter (1¾ pints) of water.

Adjusting the dose

• If the ratio is 55 g of coffee to 1 liter (1¾ pints) of water, the coffee is mild.

• If the ratio is 80 g of coffee to 1 liter (1¾ pints) of water, the coffee is stronger.

Increase or reduce the dose of coffee per liter of water to find the ratio that delivers the best result.

The extraction time

The length of time during which the coffee is in contact with the water will determine the amount of material that is extracted from the grounds and present in the final brew. A balance needs to be struck between including as many desirable elements and as few undesirable elements as possible. If the extraction time is too short, the coffee will be greatly lacking in flavor. If the extraction time is too long, the coffee will develop negative flavors in the cup.

EXTRACTION TOO SHORT

LACK OF FLAVOR

EXTRACTION TOO LONG

NEGATIVE FLAVORS

STIRRING

Stirring the coffee with a spoon or stirrer enables the water to soak all the grounds thoroughly so that all the coffee particles are extracted simultaneously. Stirring makes for faster, more uniform extraction. It can be counted as an additional parameter, provided it is done with a regular, constant motion.

The method

To understand and gauge the impact of a parameter on the final brew, the correct method is to adjust one parameter and compare the resulting different brews.

1   Start with a first coffee made using the basic parameters, then change the grind size (to either a finer or coarser grind) for the second (if you are able to brew the two coffees at the same time, that's even better). Sample, compare, and make note of which one yields the better result.

2   Stay with the grind parameter that yields the best coffee, then change the coffee/water ratio. Sample, compare, and make note of the results.

3   Stay with the coffee/water ratio that you liked the most, then try changing the temperature of the water.

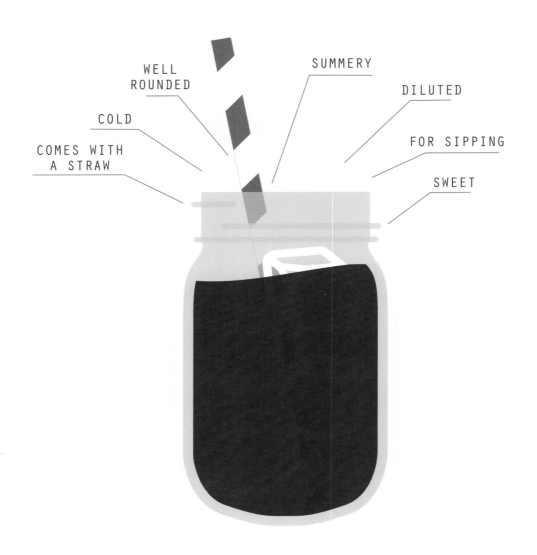

COMES WITH
A STRAW

COLD

WELL
ROUNDED

SUMMERY

DILUTED

FOR SIPPING

SWEET

COLD COFFEE

A cold coffee is brewed in just the same way as a filter coffee . . . but consumed cold. Chilled coffees are all the rage nowadays. In summer cold coffees are the cool drink to be seen with!

Hot brew

"Japanese-style" iced coffees are one of a kind, in that they are brewed hot and consumed iced! In other words, the coffee is cooled right away, ready for drinking.

Cold brew

Coffee obtained by cold brewing is very different from hot-brewed coffee. There is no sourness to speak of; the coffee is well rounded, sweet, even syrupy. Coffee shops often sell coffee produced by this method in attractively labeled bottles.

The classic cold-brew method

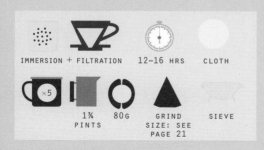

IMMERSION + FILTRATION   12–16 HRS   CLOTH

×5   1¾ PINTS   80G   GRIND SIZE: SEE PAGE 21   SIEVE

1 The day before, place the ground coffee in a lidded container, pour in water, taking care to ensure that all the grounds are thoroughly wetted, then put the lid on. Leave to steep in the refrigerator for 12 to 16 hours.

2 The next day, lay a cloth filter in a sieve and place the sieve over a pitcher. Filter the coffee and add ice cubes.

COLD BREW

The technique described below is one for budding chemists!

FILTRATION   20–24 HRS   PAPER   70–90G

1¾ PINTS   ×5   GRIND SIZE: SEE PAGE 21

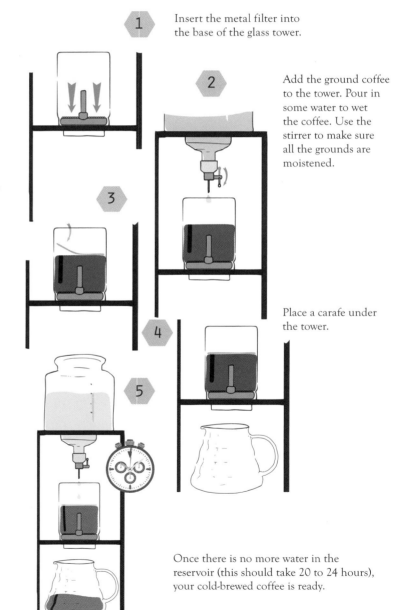

1. Insert the metal filter into the base of the glass tower.

2. Add the ground coffee to the tower. Pour in some water to wet the coffee. Use the stirrer to make sure all the grounds are moistened.

Lay the paper filter on top of the ground coffee.

3.

Place a carafe under the tower.

4.

5.

Fill the reservoir with water.

Adjust the valve so that the water flows at a rate of about 1 drop per second.

Once there is no more water in the reservoir (this should take 20 to 24 hours), your cold-brewed coffee is ready.

JAPANESE-STYLE ICED COFFEE

In an iced coffee, the melting ice cubes will partly dilute the brewed coffee. For this reason, it is preferable to use, first of all, an intensely aromatic coffee with a strong sour taste and, secondly, water of equal quality for both the brewing and the ice cubes.

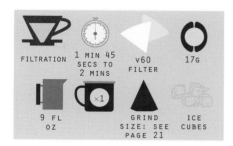

FILTRATION | 1 MIN 45 SECS TO 2 MINS | V60 FILTER | 17G

9 FL OZ | ×1 | GRIND SIZE: SEE PAGE 21 | ICE CUBES

ICED COFFEE WITH ICE CUBES... THAT DON'T MELT

You can brew an iced filter coffee using the classic coffee/water ratio—i.e., 12 to 13 g per 7 fl oz of water—provided you use reusable ice cubes containing a liquid refrigerant that will cool the beverage without diluting it. Just make sure you use plenty of them.

Heat approximately 9 fl oz of water to 201°F. If you do not have a thermometer, bring the water to a boil and leave it uncovered for 30 to 40 seconds.

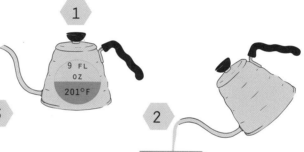

1

9 FL OZ

201°F

2

Place a filter in the Hario V60 and rinse it with 3½ fl oz of hot water. Discard the water.

3

Half fill the carafe with ice cubes. Pour in 17 g of coffee. Place the Hario V60 and the carafe on a scale. Tare the scale to zero.

4

Start the timer and pour in 50 g of hot water, taking care to moisten all of the grounds. Stir.

After 30 seconds, pour in another 50 g of water in a clockwise circular motion.

At 1 minute, pour in another 50 g of hot water.

The water will finish percolating through at around 1¾ to 2 minutes.

CHAPTER

3

ROASTING

ROASTING

Roasting involves burning the green coffee beans to unlock their flavors.
This is a complicated, subtle job, and the master roaster must have a comprehensive
understanding of the beans and his equipment. The barista also needs to have a good grasp of
roasting to enable him to select and use his beans to best effect.

The roaster

"Roaster" is the name for both the artisan and the machine that cooks the beans.
There are various types of models available, with different capacities (from 3½ oz
to several hundred pounds), power sources (gas or electricity), and designs.
The most commonly used type of roaster is a rotary cylindrical drum oven with
direct gas heating. With this type of machine, small-scale roasting takes between
10 and 20 minutes, at temperatures between 374–446°F.

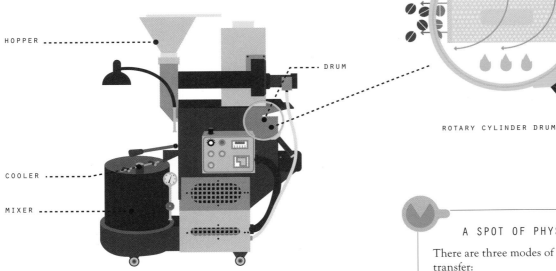

HOPPER

DRUM

COOLER

MIXER

ROTARY CYLINDER DRUM

Small-scale roasting

In a roaster, the heat is transmitted principally by convection and conduction;
radiation plays a part as well, contributing to the stability of the roasting process.
The artisan roaster controls:
• the heating power
• the intensity of the flow of air around the coffee beans (controlling convection)
• the speed of rotation of the drum, which is in direct contact with the beans
(controlling conduction)
At the end of the roasting cycle, the beans pass into the cooler, where they are
rapidly stirred and cool air from a blower is forced through them to stop them
from cooking any further.

A SPOT OF PHYSICS

There are three modes of heat
transfer:
• by convection (through a fluid)

• by conduction (through direct
contact)

• by radiation (through space)

Industrial roasting

The majority of the large-scale roasters roast their beans using fast methods (at 392°F for less than 10 minutes) or so-called "flash" methods (90 seconds at 1,472°F). These techniques do not allow the aromas and flavors to develop, and in the latter case, the beans have to be cooled in water. To ascertain whether your ground coffee has been roasted by this method, put it in the freezer: if it solidifies, that means that, unfortunately, its moisture content is at the maximum legally permitted level of 5 percent.

Home roasting

It is perfectly possible to roast your own green coffee beans at home.

What coffees should you choose?
Green coffee beans can only be purchased from certain artisan roasters. When you are buying, bear in mind that the green beans will lose between 11 and 22 percent of their mass during roasting. Choose resilient beans that are easy to manage, such as washed coffees of the bourbon, pacas, caturra, or catuai varieties.

Set yourself up with a small home roaster
Forget pan roasting, which, though accessible, is also unsatisfactory because the beans need convection and continuous mixing. You can now get small roasting machines with a batch capacity of 3 oz to 1 lb, 2 oz, which is ample for domestic consumption.

BATCH: QUANTITY OF COFFEE ROASTED AT A TIME.

FLUIDIZED BED ROASTER
A kind of slightly modified popcorn machine with a forced convection system. The only adjustable parameter is the roasting time.

DRUM ROASTER
It comes with more sophisticated heating control (temperature and time). You can expect to pay between $120 and $1,200 for one, but do not expect it to bring out the flavors and aromas as well as a commercial roaster. Nevertheless, you still have the pleasure of roasting your own beans and having freshly roasted coffee, roasted to the exact degree you choose.

THE ROASTING OF THE BEAN

These are the stages the bean goes through during the roasting process.

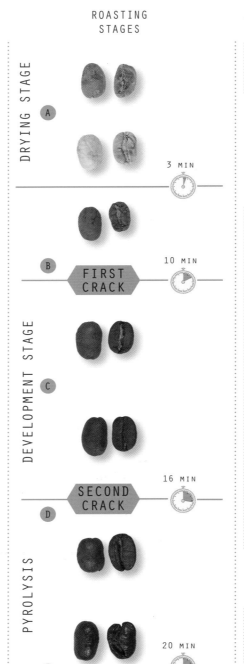

CHANGES TO THE COFFEE BEAN

The coffee bean changes from green to yellow.
The internal moisture level of the coffee bean falls.
This is an endothermic reaction: it absorbs heat.

The heat transforms the moisture within the bean into steam.
↓
Carbon dioxide (CO_2) is generated inside the bean.
↓
The pressure is increased to 25 bar.
↓
First crack:
The bean makes a characteristic cracking noise.

The bean increases in volume by 1.5 to 2 times, while losing at least 11 percent of its mass. It emits heat (exothermic reaction), turns brown (by the Strecker reaction), and sheds a layer of skin known as the silver skin, which passes into a collector.

If roasting continues, the CO_2 continues to expand.
↓
Second crack
The bean turns brown: the darker the color, the greater the roast level. The coffee can lose up to 22 percent of its mass.
The reaction is exothermic.

After the second crack, the coffee bean undergoes pyrolysis: its surface becomes oily and the bean takes on a blackened look and is liable to combust.

ROASTING STAGES

DRYING STAGE

A

3 MIN

B — FIRST CRACK — 10 MIN

DEVELOPMENT STAGE

C

SECOND CRACK — 16 MIN

D

PYROLYSIS

20 MIN

E

FLAVOR DEVELOPMENT

Three or four flavors are unlocked during the drying phase.

The flavors and aromas are unlocked by two phenomena:
• Maillard reactions: When the bean's moisture level drops below 5 percent, chemical reactions occur between the sugars and the amino acids produced by the breakdown of the proteins.
• Caramelization: A chemical reaction between the water and a sugar, saccharose.

As time goes by, the acidity diminishes and the bitterness increases. The reaction becomes endothermic again.

By the end of the roast cycle, nearly eight hundred aromas have been unlocked, as well as flavors, acidity, sweetness, and body. Sometimes undesirable roasting flavors are produced.

During this last phase, the aromas are destroyed and replaced by bitter flavors. The acidity is eliminated and the body diminishes.

Roasting and bean temperature

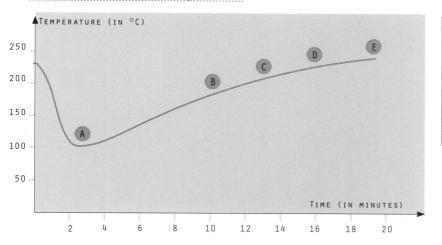

IS BEAN COLOR AN ACCURATE GUIDE?

There is no universal bean color code to define the roast level. A better method is to note the time of the first crack relative to the total roasting time.

Roasting and caffeine levels

The caffeine content of a green coffee bean (between 0.6 and 2 percent by mass for Arabica beans) remains virtually unchanged during roasting, regardless of the roast level (caffeine content falls by about 10 percent).

However, the longer the roasting goes on, the more the mass of the coffee decreases (a fall of between 11 and 22 percent), so the caffeine level naturally increases.

The trend is toward an ever-lighter roast

Beyond a certain roasting point, the coffee's aromas are masked by the roasting flavors (caramel, followed by smoky, bitter, and burnt); only a light roast allows the coffee aromas to be preserved.

The roaster has to compromise when it comes to the taste characteristics he wants to emphasize. For example, if he is looking for greater acidity, combined with a broad spectrum of flavors, this will probably be at the expense of the body.

TANGY IS GOOD!

This moderate roast has the effect of bringing out the natural acidity of the beans. The heat applied during roasting largely destroys the forty or so chlorogenic acids (the famous polyphenols regarded as good acids), which break down into quinic and caffeic acid, two astringent compounds. The majority of the other organic acids, like citric and malic acid, reach their peak concentration with a light roast, then steadily decrease.

This explains why a fast, light roast will produce beans with greater acidity potential.

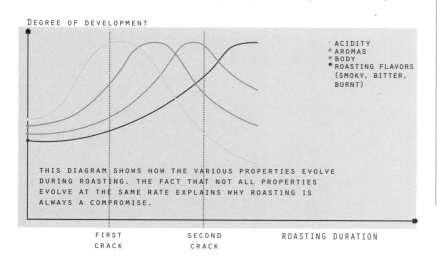

DEGREE OF DEVELOPMENT

ACIDITY
AROMAS
BODY
ROASTING FLAVORS (SMOKY, BITTER, BURNT)

THIS DIAGRAM SHOWS HOW THE VARIOUS PROPERTIES EVOLVE DURING ROASTING. THE FACT THAT NOT ALL PROPERTIES EVOLVE AT THE SAME RATE EXPLAINS WHY ROASTING IS ALWAYS A COMPROMISE.

FIRST CRACK   SECOND CRACK   ROASTING DURATION

ROASTING STYLES

To produce a good coffee, there is more than one way to roast the beans.
The master roaster, by adjusting the bean temperature and roasting time,
creates a blend of flavors and aromas that is tailored for each coffee.

Roast profiles

Each green coffee bean has its own flavor and aroma potential shaped by its terroir, its variety, its cultivation method, and its processing. It is the job of the master roaster to unlock this potential. The heating time and temperature do not on their own define the roast, since the roast is a matter of more than just cooking, and requires specific temperature variations, known as roast profiles. By playing with these profiles, the artisan roaster can emphasize one quality or another (onset, acidity, aromas, body, sweetness, finish, etc.). Hence, two identical green coffee beans can yield two totally different brews, one more acidic, the other with more pronounced spicy aromas, with a fuller body, and so on. The roaster "interprets" his coffee and stamps his own style on it.

Beware: Appearance can be deceiving!

If you have two beans roasted to the same color, does it mean their roasting profile is the same? No, a profile is not defined by either the final color of the bean or identical start and end temperatures, and certainly not by the final brew. The final color of the bean is merely an indicator of the point at which roasting ceased. The roast profile is the journey it took to get there. Depending on the roast profile for each, these two apparently identical beans will each give a very different brew.

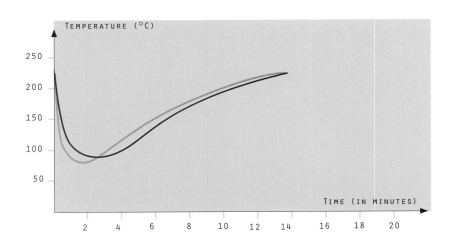

THE TWO CURVES REPRESENT ROAST PROFILES. THEY HAVE THE SAME STARTING POINT AND THE SAME END POINT, AND YET THE RESULTING DRINKS, BREWED IN THE SAME WAY, WILL BE DIFFERENT.

The right roasting style for every purpose

Some beans need to be roasted differently for different brewing methods, whereas others can cope perfectly well with a single roasting style.

Factor 1: The bean
Certain beans are better suited to certain brewing methods. In this case, roasters offer a single roast option; it is up to the barista to alter the brewing method according to the selected coffee.

Factor 2: The brewing method
The preparation method determines the balance of flavors. The same coffee, depending on the chosen method, will develop bitterness after three minutes' steeping in the case of a filter coffee, or sourness after a 20- to 30-second extraction in the case of an espresso. To compensate for the sour/bitter imbalance, some roasters offer specially tailored roasts for each brewing method.

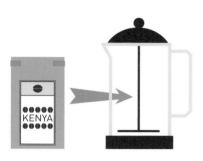

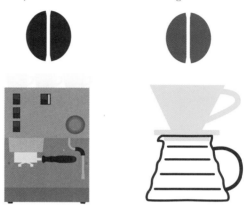

THE SAME BEAN, BUT A SPECIFIC ROAST STYLE FOR EACH BREWING METHOD

Factor 3: The consumer
Every country has its own consumption and roasting habits. The Scandinavian countries, for example, which are keen on filter coffee, prefer light-roast coffees, whereas the Mediterranean countries use dark-roasted beans for their espressos. This variation is even visible within a single country: southern Italy uses much darker beans than those used in the north of the country.

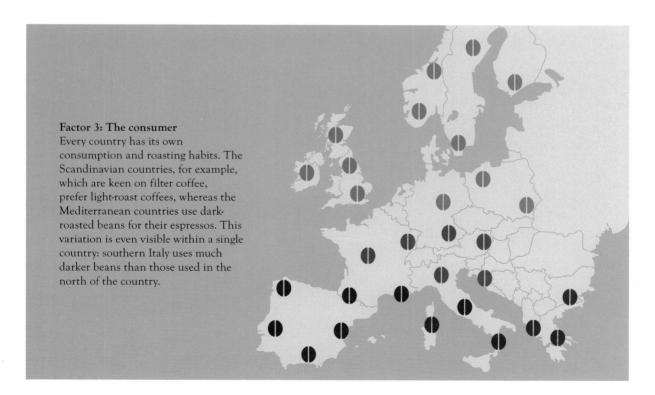

BLEND OR SINGLE ORIGIN?

There are two kinds of coffee out there:
coffee from a single origin and coffee that is a blend of several origins.

Single origin

There are various definitions of "single origin." The one most commonly accepted defines single origin as referring to beans from a single terroir—for example, beans harvested on a single farm. By extension, coffee harvested on several farms but pooled at the same washing station can be deemed single origin as well.

Single origin presents a unique, typical character that the experienced taster will be able to appreciate: through the bean, he can recognize and assess the terroir (soil type, climate, exposure, etc.) as well as the work that has gone into the cultivation, harvesting, and drying.

EXTRA PURE? YES, BUT ...

For some "purists," single origin not only has to come from a single terroir, it also has to be mono-varietal; in other words, it can only comprise a single coffee variety. This extreme requirement is of dubious value, particularly given that it would prevent the farmer from practicing sustainable agriculture. It is important that the farmer is able to cultivate several varieties. This enables him to pick varieties suited to the different altitudes on his land and limit the risk of his entire crop being hit by a disease or parasite, but it also means a particular taste can be achieved by mixing varieties.

The blend

A blend is a combination of coffees of different origins (regions, countries ...). The big companies generally blend their coffee, as it enables them to harmonize the flavor of the coffee and offer consumers a consistent taste by adjusting the proportions of the coffees in the blend. Not only that, but when done well, the blend can also be better than the coffees of which it is composed.

Which package for which brewing method?

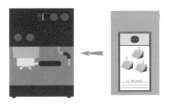

Espresso is a temperamental process! That is why it is safer to use a blend: this maximizes the chances of obtaining a consistent coffee that is undemanding, balanced, and easy to make. In the right dose, the blend combines the qualities of the various coffees (sweetness in the case of Brazil, acidity and aromas for Ethiopia, etc.) and compensates for the numerous difficulties associated with this process, as well as the instability of domestic

espresso machines. Slow methods bring out the subtleties of the finest coffees; so the specialty coffees intended for slow-brew methods are generally single origin. Nevertheless, some roasters offer blends for slow brewing to develop a richer array of flavors.

CREATING YOUR OWN BLEND

Anyone can concoct their own blend! There are just three steps to it (defining your objective, choosing your varieties, and working out the right proportions); everything else comes down to your taste.

Defining your objective

Before putting together a blend, you first have to establish what kind of brew it is intended for (espresso, cappuccino, filter, etc.), as well as the characteristics you want to achieve (flavor complexity, body, fruitiness, balance …).

CUPPING FOR THE PROS

"Cupping" is the professional technique whereby the coffees (see pages 118–119) are "cupped" one by one in order to appraise them and identify the ways in which they might complement one another.

Choosing countries of origin

THE COFFEES OF CENTRAL AMERICA

Costa Rican, Salvadorian, or Guatemalan beans make excellent single-source espressos.
Qualities: Flavor complexity and acidity.
Proportion: The best beans are able to stand on their own.
Result: Balanced coffees with many qualities.

ASIAN COFFEES

Qualities: Body (Vietnamese, Indonesian), flavors, and particular features such as the iodized notes and incredible crema of the Monsoon Malabar (see page 171).

THE COFFEES OF SOUTH AMERICA

Good base for blends for espresso.
Qualities: Sweetness, body, clarity, moderate acidity, relatively neutral flavor base.
Proportion: High (some blends are composed entirely of South American coffees).
Result: A consensus blend that is accessible and, above all, easier to extract.

AFRICAN COFFEES

Qualities: Demonstrative, with fruity and floral aromas, acidity (the Kenyans score most highly for this), and nice flavor complexity.
Result: Less body, except maybe for some Tanzanian coffees, which, in some respects, resemble the coffees of Central America (Guatemalan coffee, for example).

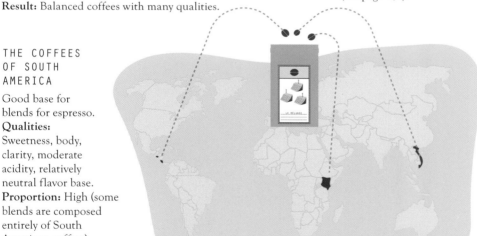

Getting the proportions right

Limit yourself to no more than three or four coffees in your blend. Any more, and the qualities of each will become diluted and the blend will lose its personality.

Start by having all the origins in equal proportions (50/50 for two origins; 30/30/30 for three origins, etc.):

• If one of the origins is dominating the others
→ halve its proportion.
• If one of the coffees is too muted
→ double its proportion.
Example of a blend:
50% Brazil / 25% Guatemala / 25% Ethiopia

READING A COFFEE PACKAGE

Of course coffee can be bought from all kinds of outlets, from supermarkets to coffee shops, not to mention roasting houses themselves or specialist websites. To ensure you end up with the coffee that best meets your expectations, it is useful to be able to interpret the information on the package …

Decoding the label

The label on a package of coffee provides the information you need to help you pick a quality coffee.

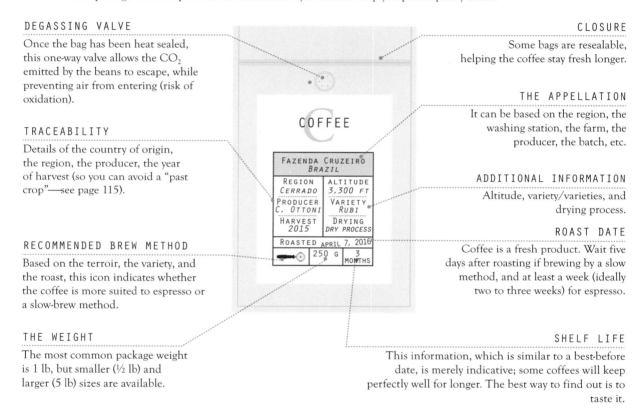

DEGASSING VALVE
Once the bag has been heat sealed, this one-way valve allows the CO_2 emitted by the beans to escape, while preventing air from entering (risk of oxidation).

TRACEABILITY
Details of the country of origin, the region, the producer, the year of harvest (so you can avoid a "past crop"—see page 115).

RECOMMENDED BREW METHOD
Based on the terroir, the variety, and the roast, this icon indicates whether the coffee is more suited to espresso or a slow-brew method.

THE WEIGHT
The most common package weight is 1 lb, but smaller (½ lb) and larger (5 lb) sizes are available.

CLOSURE
Some bags are resealable, helping the coffee stay fresh longer.

THE APPELLATION
It can be based on the region, the washing station, the farm, the producer, the batch, etc.

ADDITIONAL INFORMATION
Altitude, variety/varieties, and drying process.

ROAST DATE
Coffee is a fresh product. Wait five days after roasting if brewing by a slow method, and at least a week (ideally two to three weeks) for espresso.

SHELF LIFE
This information, which is similar to a best-before date, is merely indicative; some coffees will keep perfectly well for longer. The best way to find out is to taste it.

Label content:

COFFEE

FAZENDA CRUZEIRO
BRAZIL

REGION *CERRADO*	ALTITUDE *3,300 FT*
PRODUCER *C. OTTONI*	VARIETY *RUBI*
HARVEST *2015*	DRYING *DRY PROCESS*

ROASTED *APRIL 7, 2016*

250 G | 3 MONTHS

Beware of marketing ploys

"Coffee strength"
Unless it comes with further explanation, this term (accompanied by a number scale or terms like full-bodied, sweet, etc.) is little more than marketing speak and tells us little about the coffee's flavor profile. The coffee's strength is a function of the dose of grounds and the process used to brew it, so it depends on the manner of preparation. On packaging destined for the mass market, strength is essentially synonymous with "roast level" or "grind fineness"—in other words, it is used to mean bitterness.

"100% Arabica"
A good coffee will always be Arabica.

"Slow-roasted"
Certainly, slow roasting is better than flash roasting, but this doesn't tell you whether the roast profile is a successful one. The fact is, a twelve-minute roast can, depending on the profile, give better results than an eighteen-minute roast. So slowness is not necessarily synonymous with quality.

PURCHASING SPECIALTY COFFEE

Ready-ground coffee may well not give satisfactory quality or last long before it deteriorates.
Only the coffee specialists are in a position to provide coffee that is fresh and correctly roasted.

From the roaster

The roaster is a passionate artisan who can provide information on roasting dates, cultivation conditions, flavor profiles, and the brewing methods to which the beans are best suited. He is able to provide advice and tailor his products to the customer's needs, right down to the desired grind size.

IDENTIFYING A GOOD ROASTER

1 The coffees are protected from the ambient air, in a silo or other containers for this purpose.
2 The roasted coffee beans on offer are a fairly light brown, indicating a carefully managed roast.
3 The list of available coffees should not be too long (fifteen maximum). This ensures the beans are fresh and roast profiles are well managed.

ROASTERS TO AVOID

1 Bags of green coffee strewn around the floor, or in a window, show that storage conditions are not ideal; this is likely to shorten the shelf life of the coffee.
2 Does the date of harvest indicate an old harvest? This is what is known as a "past crop."
3 The roasted coffee beans are dark, with shiny traces of caffeol: the roast time was too long and the coffee is likely to be bitter.

In coffee shops

Baristas work in close collaboration with roasters and sell excellent-quality coffee, which you can sometimes sample on the premises. They can give information on the various coffees, since it is they who selected them, and on the recommended brewing methods. Make the most of them!

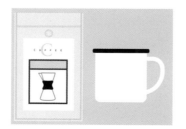

CUP OF EXCELLENCE

These are national competitions set up in 1999 by coffee connoisseurs in association with the governments of the producer countries and NGOs. The coffees are sampled by an international tasting panel, and the winning coffees are put up for auction in real time on the Internet. The producer benefits from the boost to his reputation, and for the consumer, the Cup of Excellence designation is a guarantee of a balanced, quality coffee.

STORING COFFEE AT HOME

Green coffee is a delicate product that does not store well. Once roasted, it is even more fragile.
To preserve its flavors as best as possible, there are a few simple measures the consumer should take.

Nonperishable but fragile

Coffee is a "nonperishable" product, which is to say that there is no risk if you consume it after the best-before date, unlike "perishable" goods, which must carry a use-by date that must not be exceeded. After the best-before date (BBD), only the sensory and nutritional qualities of the coffee are no longer guaranteed. Whether the coffee is in the form of beans or ground, the storage advice is identical. However, ground coffee degrades even more quickly because it has a larger surface area in contact with the air, and grinding causes the release of CO_2, which acts naturally to preserve the bean (its pressure creates a barrier to the oxygen.

> **COFFEE DOES NOT LIKE**
> - high temperatures
> - oxygen
> - moisture
> - excessive dryness
> - light

Where to store

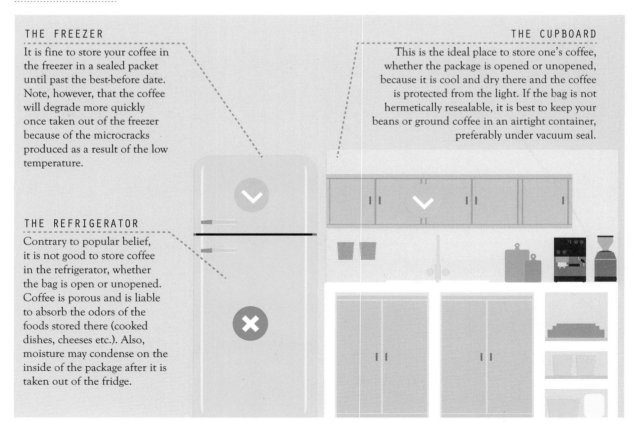

THE FREEZER

It is fine to store your coffee in the freezer in a sealed packet until past the best-before date. Note, however, that the coffee will degrade more quickly once taken out of the freezer because of the microcracks produced as a result of the low temperature.

THE CUPBOARD

This is the ideal place to store one's coffee, whether the package is opened or unopened, because it is cool and dry there and the coffee is protected from the light. If the bag is not hermetically resealable, it is best to keep your beans or ground coffee in an airtight container, preferably under vacuum seal.

THE REFRIGERATOR

Contrary to popular belief, it is not good to store coffee in the refrigerator, whether the bag is open or unopened. Coffee is porous and is liable to absorb the odors of the foods stored there (cooked dishes, cheeses etc.). Also, moisture may condense on the inside of the package after it is taken out of the fridge.

Types of package

Coffee packaging has evolved over time with the aim of helping the coffee stay fresh for as long as possible.

SEALED BROWN PAPER OR MULTILAYER BAGS

 The
+ • THE SIMPLEST AND LEAST EXPENSIVE

 The
− • NO VALVE. THEY DO NOT ALLOW THE COFFEE TO DEGAS NATURALLY.
• SHELF LIFE COULD BE BETTER.

BBD NOT STATED

HERMETICALLY SEALED, RESEALABLE BAGS, FITTED WITH A DEPRESSURIZATION VALVE.

 The
+ • GOOD AT KEEPING COFFEE FRESH
• RESEALABLE

 The
− EXPENSIVE

USED BY THE MAJORITY OF ARTISANAL ROASTERS, WHO ARE KEEN TO PRESERVE THE FRESHNESS OF THEIR COFFEE.

BBD UP TO 3 MONTHS IN AN UNOPENED BAG. ONCE OPENED, THE COFFEE WILL GO STALE WITHIN A FEW DAYS.

BAGS OR CANS UNDER NITROGEN PRESSURE

 USED BY LARGE ARTISANAL ROASTERS AND/OR INDUSTRIAL-SCALE COMPANIES.

The
+ • THE BEST AT KEEPING COFFEE FRESH
• NITROGEN, A NEUTRAL GAS, REPLACES THE OXYGEN THAT CAUSES THE OXIDATION OF OILS
• A DEGASSING VALVE

The
− SUBSTANTIAL INVESTMENT AND LOGISTICS REQUIREMENTS FOR THE ROASTER

BBD MUCH LONGER—UP TO A YEAR

VACUUM-SEALED BAGS WITH OR WITHOUT A VALVE

  USED MAINLY BY INDUSTRIAL-SCALE COMPANIES

The
+ • GOOD AT KEEPING COFFEE FRESH

The
− • SOME OF THE VOLATILE AROMAS ARE SUCKED OUT DURING THE PROCESS.
• NONRESEALABE

BBD UP TO 3 MONTHS IN AN UNOPENED BAG. ONCE OPENED, THE COFFEE WILL GO STALE WITHIN A FEW DAYS.

CUPPING

In order to gauge the quality and consistency of a batch of coffee, big companies have developed a standardized tasting method known as "cupping." It is a practice that you can easily play around with at home as a way of discovering different coffees.

Cupping: What is it?

Cupping involves evaluating a quantity of infused, unfiltered ground coffee in order to:
- assess the quality and the flavor profile of a batch of coffee by testing one or more samples;
- detect any defects;
- create blends.

This technique is vital in helping green coffee buyers make their choices (see page 12).

Equipment and parameters

For the sake of efficiency and to enable the various professionals involved (producers, green-coffee buyers, roasters) to communicate effectively, cupping must be performed in strict compliance with the brewing parameters laid down in an international standard.

7 FL OZ CUPPING BOWLS OR GLASSES

CUPPING SPOONS (ROUND SOUPSPOONS WITH A CAPACITY OF 8 TO 10 ML. MADE OF SILVER SO THE HEAT DISSIPATES QUICKLY.)

SCALE:
12 G OF EACH COFFEE TO BE TESTED IN THE FORM OF BEANS READY FOR GRINDING

GRINDER

KETTLE CONTAINING 7 FL OZ OF MINERAL WATER, HEATED BETWEEN 198–203°F

TIMER:
INFUSION TIME 4 MINUTES

CUPPING FORMS

The method

Evaluating the dry grounds

Grind a dose of coffee in a grinder (filter grind), then smell the volatile aromas that are released. Are they pleasant, fragrant or not? What do they evoke? This step is a short one because it is not possible to capture the volatile aromas. Between grindings, purge the grinder by grinding a few beans of the next coffee to be evaluated.

Evaluating the wet grounds

Pour the hot water onto the grounds and set the timer. The grounds will float to the surface and form a crust. Allow the coffee aromas to develop in contact with the water for 4 minutes.

Break the crust with the back of the cupping spoon and stir three times. Position your nose just above the bowl at that moment and breathe in the gases that had been trapped by the crust until then.

Some of the grounds will have sunk to the bottom of the bowl. Scoop off those remaining on the surface with a spoon, making sure to rinse it each time in a glass of water—particularly when you are going between two cupping bowls containing different coffees.

CUPPING FORM

As with any assessment, it is vital to make a note of your findings and sensations during the course of the tasting. You can get relatively comprehensive forms covering the following criteria:

Taste the coffee, at different temperatures, until it is cold. Use a cupping spoon to take a little coffee from the bowl, inhale deeply to make sure the aromas reach the whole of your tongue, enabling you to better identify them by means of retronasal olfaction. Analyze both the aromas and the tactile sensations in the mouth. Is the coffee thick and creamy, or watery, like a tea? Is the aftertaste pleasant, and does it last or quickly disappear?

Aromas (dry grounds): 1–5
Notes: grass, cereals, nuts, orchard fruits, red fruits, tropical fruits . . .
Aromas (wet grounds): 1–5
Notes: grass, cereals, nuts, orchard fruits, red fruits, tropical fruits . . .
Flavors: 1–5
Notes: grass, cereals, nuts, orchard fruits, red fruits, tropical fruits . . .
Length of finish: 1–5
Acidity: 1–5
Intensity (mild to intense)
Body: 1–5
Level (thin to heavy)
Uniformity : 1–5
Balance: 1–5
Clean cup: 1–5
Sweetness: 1–5

THE FLAVOR WHEEL

The wheel helps the taster to identify the flavors and aromas of the coffee. It can be used on its own, or in conjunction with a universal lexicon known as the Sensory Lexicon, describing each aroma and flavor, its intensity, and the method by which it was obtained

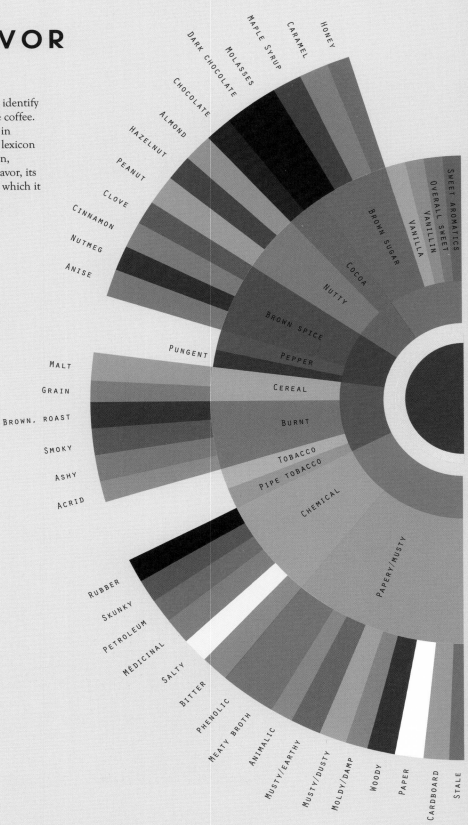

HONEY
CARAMEL
MAPLE SYRUP
MOLASSES
DARK CHOCOLATE
CHOCOLATE
ALMOND
HAZELNUT
PEANUT
CLOVE
CINNAMON
NUTMEG
ANISE

SWEET AROMATICS
OVERALL SWEET
VANILLIN
VANILLA
BROWN SUGAR
COCOA
NUTTY
BROWN SPICE
PEPPER
CEREAL
BURNT
TOBACCO
PIPE TOBACCO
CHEMICAL

PUNGENT
MALT
GRAIN
BROWN, ROAST
SMOKY
ASHY
ACRID

PAPERY/MUSTY

RUBBER
SKUNKY
PETROLEUM
MEDICINAL
SALTY
BITTER
PHENOLIC
MEATY BROTH
ANIMALIC
MUSTY/EARTHY
MUSTY/DUSTY
MOLDY/DAMP
WOODY
PAPER
CARDBOARD
STALE

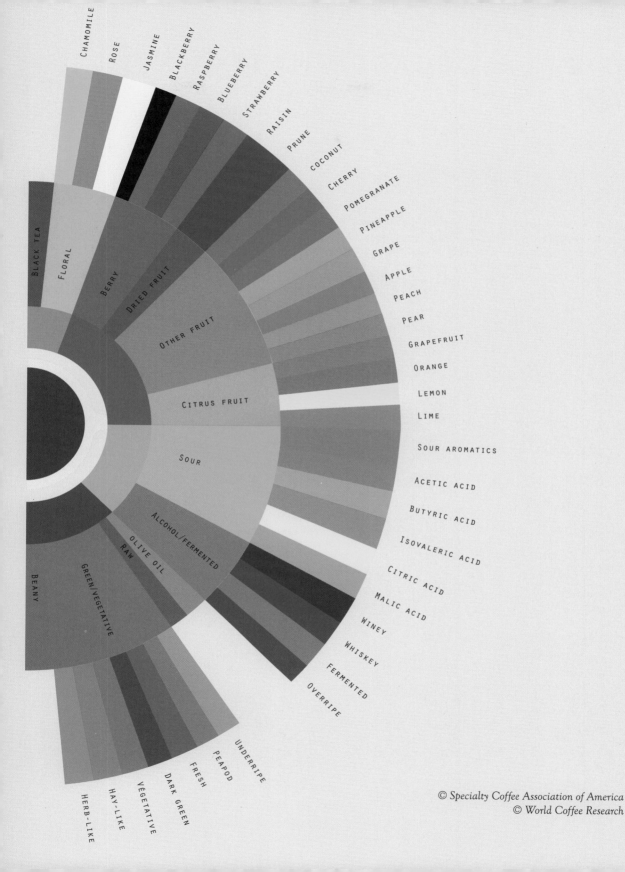

CHAMOMILE
ROSE
JASMINE
BLACKBERRY
RASPBERRY
BLUEBERRY
STRAWBERRY
RAISIN
PRUNE
COCONUT
CHERRY
POMEGRANATE
PINEAPPLE
GRAPE
APPLE
PEACH
PEAR
GRAPEFRUIT
ORANGE
LEMON
LIME
SOUR AROMATICS
ACETIC ACID
BUTYRIC ACID
ISOVALERIC ACID
CITRIC ACID
MALIC ACID
WINEY
WHISKEY
FERMENTED
OVERRIPE
UNDERRIPE
PEAPOD
FRESH
DARK GREEN
VEGETATIVE
HAY-LIKE
HERB-LIKE

BLACK TEA
FLORAL
BERRY
DRIED FRUIT
OTHER FRUIT
CITRUS FRUIT
SOUR
ALCOHOL/FERMENTED
OLIVE OIL
RAW
GREEN/VEGETATIVE
BEANY

© Specialty Coffee Association of America
© World Coffee Research

DECAFFEINATION

One of coffee's foremost properties is that it stimulates the brain and heightens alertness, but these qualities also cause negative effects for some consumers. To counter this problem, various processes have been developed for decaffeinating coffee.

The principle

Caffeine was discovered in 1819 by a German chemist, Friedlieb Ferdinand Runge. And as early as the end of the nineteenth century, research was conducted into ways of limiting its effects or even eliminating it altogether while still preserving the coffee's other components. Since the time the first method was devised in 1903 by a coffee merchant, Ludwig Roselius, the processes have moved on a great deal, but they are still performed on green coffee beans, making them difficult to roast, and altering their flavors.

Decaffeination using chemical solvents (conventional method)

There are two methods involving the use of solvents.

Direct method

 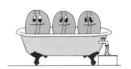  

1 The green coffee beans are steamed or immersed in hot water to open their pores.

2 The solvent is added and decaffeination begins.

3 The beans are then washed to remove, as far as possible, any traces of solvent.

4 The beans are dried and ready for roasting.

Indirect method
The coffee beans do not come into direct contact with the solvent.

1 The green coffee beans are first immersed in very hot water, which extracts all the soluble elements contained within them.

2 The beans are removed from the water, which is now saturated with these elements, and the water is poured into another tank together with the solvent, which will fix the caffeine.

3 The water is heated to drive off the caffeine-laden solvent by evaporation.

4 The green coffee beans are immersed in the water again, and all the components extracted at the first stage are reintroduced into the beans.

Decaffeination using water: the Swiss Water Process (SWP)

This method does not use chemical solvents. Pioneered in 1933, it was introduced to the market in the 1980s and is patented as the Swiss Water Process.

1 A batch of green coffee beans is immersed in very hot water to extract the caffeine and all the desirable flavor components from them.

2 The water saturated with all these substances is passed through a charcoal filter that captures only the caffeine molecules, which are larger than the others. The batch of green coffee stripped of its caffeine, flavors, and other desirable substances is discarded.

3 A second batch of green coffee is immersed in the water that is carrying the soluble substances from the first batch of green coffee, which is now able to absorb only the caffeine. The flavor components of the second batch will therefore remain in the beans.

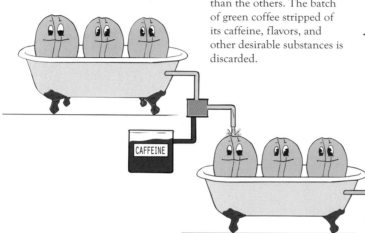

4 The water is then refiltered to remove the caffeine so it is ready to receive a third batch of green coffee. The second batch is then dried.

Decaffeination with CO_2

This is the newest method. It uses CO_2 at a temperature of 88°F and at very high pressure (200 bar), which makes it nearly as dense as water; it is known as supercritical carbon dioxide (CO_2).

1 The beans are soaked in water in a tank.

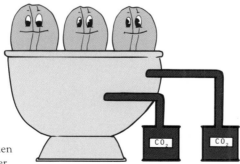

2 Supercritical CO_2 is introduced to extract the caffeine. Several cycles are needed for decaffeination to be effective, but this process has the advantage of being more selective than others in its extraction of the caffeine.

3 The caffeine-laden CO_2 is then transferred to another container where the pressure is released and the CO_2 returns to its gaseous state, leaving the caffeine behind.

4 The decaffeinated coffee beans are dried.

4

CULTIVATION

COFFEE CULTIVATION

Before it is crafted into a drink, coffee takes the form of a green bean extracted from the fruit of the coffee plant. Like cocoa, this is an exotic agricultural product that can only be grown in certain parts of the world.

The coffee cherry

Coffee beans are the seeds contained in the "cherries" of the coffee plant. Each cherry normally contains two beans, but it sometimes happens that it only contains a single one (which is then called a peaberry or caracole) or none at all, or even more than two beans.

The cherry, which starts off green, takes on a red or yellow or orange color as it ripens, depending on the variety.

THE PARCHMENT

The parchment is a hard layer surrounding the bean in the coffee cherry. Its job is to protect the bean.

THE MUCILAGE

The mucilage is the slimy part of the pulp attached to the parchment.

A POTTED HISTORY

According to some theories, coffee can be traced back to the high plateaus of Ethiopia in the days of the ancient kingdom of Abyssinia. It is not possible to attribute a precise date to humanity's discovery of the coffee plant, but it appears that the Ethiopians used to use the pulp of the coffee cherries to make juice. According to some sources, coffee crossed the Red Sea in the tenth century, and was prized for its mind-stimulating effect in the Arab-Muslim world, where the consumption of alcohol was forbidden. It reached the Ottoman empire in the fifteenth century, and was introduced to the West in the seventeenth century.

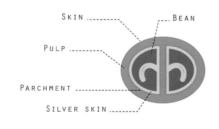

SKIN · · · · · · BEAN

PULP · · · · · ·

PARCHMENT · · · · · ·

SILVER SKIN · · · · · ·

TRANSVERSE SECTION

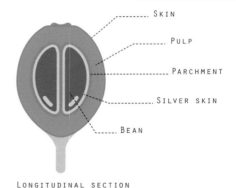

· · · · · · SKIN

· · · · · · PULP

· · · · · · PARCHMENT

· · · · · · SILVER SKIN

· · · · · · BEAN

LONGITUDINAL SECTION

A modest yield!

A coffee plant produces between 3 and 5½ lb of cherries a year (some varieties are more productive than others). These contain between 9 and 17 oz of green coffee beans, which will yield 7 to 13 oz of roasted coffee. All in all, one coffee plant on its own produces very little coffee, sometimes less than half a 1-lb bag of coffee!

1 COFFEE PLANT

=

3 LB < CHERRIES / YEAR < 5 ½ LB

=

7 OZ < ROASTED COFFEE < 13 OZ

Growing conditions for *Coffea arabica*

It is in the tropical belt between the Tropics of Cancer and Capricorn that *Coffea arabica* is cultivated.

Subtropical zone
In the subtropical zone, coffee is grown at altitudes of between 2,000 and 4,000 ft. The wet and dry seasons are clearly distinct, allowing only one harvest.

Tropical zone
In the tropical zone, coffee is grown at altitudes of between 4,000 and 8,000 ft. The much more frequent rain causes the coffee plants to flower continuously, allowing two harvests (one during the very rainy season, and a second, smaller harvest in the less rainy season).

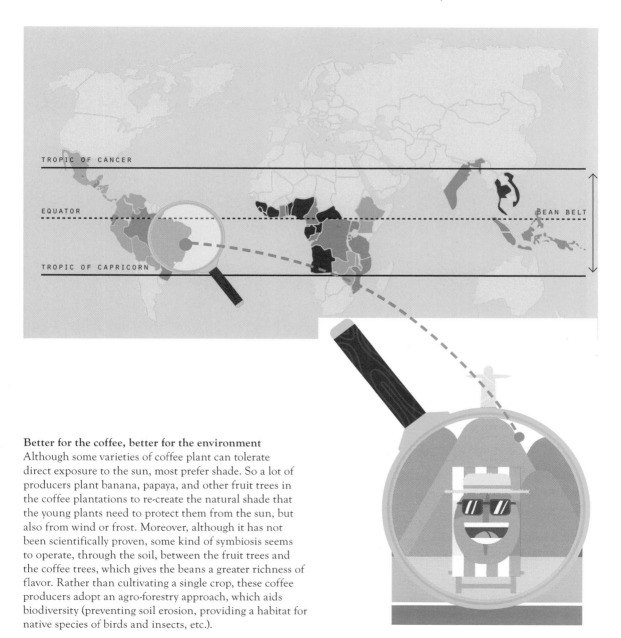

Better for the coffee, better for the environment
Although some varieties of coffee plant can tolerate direct exposure to the sun, most prefer shade. So a lot of producers plant banana, papaya, and other fruit trees in the coffee plantations to re-create the natural shade that the young plants need to protect them from the sun, but also from wind or frost. Moreover, although it has not been scientifically proven, some kind of symbiosis seems to operate, through the soil, between the fruit trees and the coffee trees, which gives the beans a greater richness of flavor. Rather than cultivating a single crop, these coffee producers adopt an agro-forestry approach, which aids biodiversity (preventing soil erosion, providing a habitat for native species of birds and insects, etc.).

LIFE CYCLE
OF A COFFEE PLANT

A coffee producer just starting out will need to be patient, since a coffee plant does not produce its first cherries for at least three years, and in some cases up to five years.

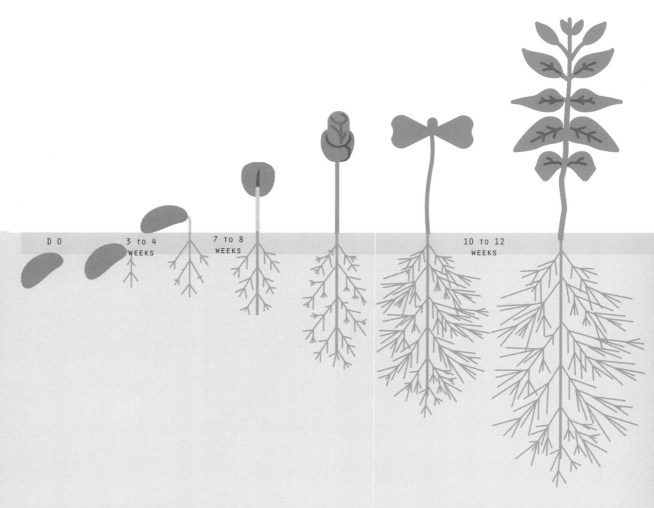

D 0

3 TO 4
WEEKS

7 TO 8
WEEKS

10 TO 12
WEEKS

From seed to cherry

In the right conditions, it takes between three and four weeks for the seed of the coffee tree to germinate. The roots appear, then a stem capped with parchment emerges from the ground three or four weeks later. After ten to twelve weeks, the parchment falls off, giving way to leaves, which grow in opposite pairs and are dark green in color. It takes three to five years for the coffee tree to produce its first cherries.

16 TO 24 IN

7 TO 10 FT

3 TO 5 YEARS

6 TO 9 MONTHS

Flowering

Flowering takes place after rain, and it takes six to nine months for the fruits to reach maturity and be ready for harvesting. If the first rain is not continuous, the fruits do not all ripen at the same speed. That is why red cherries and green cherries can be found on the same branch. It means the cherries have to be carefully hand-picked in several rounds to ensure the cherries are all ripe when harvested.

CHERRIES AT DIFFERENT STAGES OF MATURITY ON ONE BRANCH

THE EARLY SOWER GETS THE COFFEE ...

The germination rate of the seeds of the coffee plant declines over time: from 95 percent for seeds stored for less than three months, to 75 percent after three months, dropping to 25 percent after nine months, and falling to zero after fifteen months. The 95 percent germination rate can be extended to six months by storing the seeds in vacuum-sealed bags at 59°F.

MORE ABOUT COFFEE GROWING

So we've covered the basics with our look at the life cycle of the coffee plant. But there are also all kinds of details and practicalities to be considered when it comes to coffee cultivation.

Propagation

There are two ways of propagating new coffee plants: by taking cuttings or by sowing the seeds.

Cuttings

This involves cutting off a small piece of the coffee plant (the tip of a branch with two leaves on it, and each leaf cut in half) and planting it. When new leaves and roots form, the cutting has taken, and develops in the same way as a seedling. Since taking cuttings is a form of cloning, each new plant will be genetically identical to the plant from which the cutting was taken.

Seeds

To obtain seeds for planting, coffee cherries are selected at full maturity, as this gives the best chances of germination. They are pulped and left to ferment for a short time (less than ten hours) before being dried and prepared for planting. The seeds are sown in containers, often polyethylene bags, in compost conducive to the growth of the young coffee plant (crumbly, light texture, fertile).

In nurseries

Seedlings and cuttings are generally grown in nurseries, rather than on a plantation itself, so as to provide a controlled, better protected environment (shelter, shade, irrigation). When the young plants are strong enough and have grown to a height of between 15 and 25 inches, with about ten pairs of leaves, they can be transplanted into the fields to continue growing.

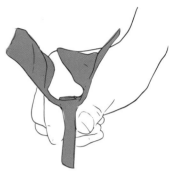

COFFEE CUTTING

NURSERY ON A COFFEE PLANTATION

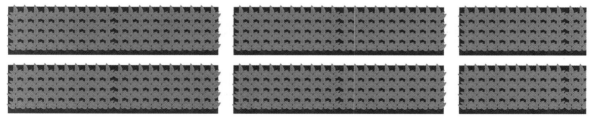

WHAT ABOUT POLLINATION?

Pollination is essentially accomplished by the wind, since *Coffea arabica* is a self-pollinating shrub. Insects only play a minor role in fertilization (between 5 and 10 percent).

Coffee flavors by altitude

The cooler climate at high altitude causes the cherries to ripen more slowly, resulting in denser beans. Broadly speaking, this means that the higher the altitude at which the coffee is growing, the greater its acidity, the fuller its aromas, and the better its taste.

THE INFLUENCE OF ALTITIUDE ON THE FLAVOR:

5,000–6,500 FT: FLORAL, SPICY, FRUITY, ACIDIC, GREATER COMPLEXITY

4,000–5,000 FT: WELL-DEVELOPED ACIDITY, MORE AROMAS

3,300–4,000 FT: LOW ACIDITY, ROUNDNESS

2,600–3,300 FT: NO ACIDITY, LITTLE COMPLEXITY

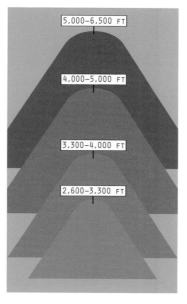

5,000–6,500 FT

4,000–5,000 FT

3,300–4,000 FT

2,600–3,300 FT

Growing organic coffee

Organic farming is relatively rare in coffee-producing countries, where the use of pesticides is the norm. Unfortunately, from a flavor perspective, organic cultivation does not enhance the quality of the brew. Therefore, flavor does not count as a reason for a farmer to change his approach. However, in some countries like Ethiopia, small-scale growers do not use any inputs because they are too expensive, which means that they practice organic farming by default, without being officially certified. In Brazil, the world's number one coffee-producing country, some producers, like Fazenda Ambiental Fortaleza, grow coffee by organic methods.

Enemies of the coffee plant

There are various natural organisms that attack *Coffea arabica*, but its two biggest enemies are the fungus that causes coffee leaf rust (*Hemileia vastatrix*), and the coffee borer beetle (*Hypothenemus hampei*).

Coffee leaf rust
Discovered in Sri Lanka in the nineteenth century, coffee leaf rust is now found in virtually all coffee-producing countries. It attacks the leaves during rainy periods, preventing photosynthesis and even causing the leaves to drop off. The coffee plant is weakened and its growth may come to a halt. To combat this disease, which takes a heavy toll on a harvest, growers can opt for more resistant hybrid varieties.

The coffee borer beetle
The coffee berry borer is a small beetle (the female is 2.5 mm long and the male, 1.5 mm). Originally from Africa, today it is found in most of the coffee-producing countries. The female bores tunnels in the coffee cherries while they are still green and lays her eggs in them. The larvae then feed on the seeds contained in the cherry.

A LEAF AFFECTED BY COFFEE LEAF RUST

A COFFEE BORER BEETLE

COFFEE VARIETIES

Over the centuries in which coffee—or Arabica, to be precise—has been cultivated, different varieties have developed. To ensure cost-effective production and good results in the cup, it is important to have a sound knowledge of the varieties and their potential in a particular terroir.

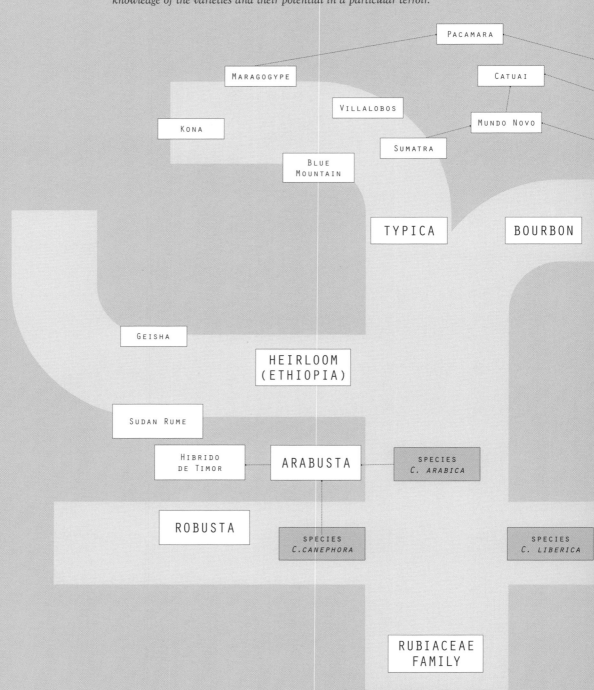

PACAMARA

MARAGOGYPE

CATUAI

VILLALOBOS

MUNDO NOVO

KONA

SUMATRA

BLUE MOUNTAIN

TYPICA

BOURBON

GEISHA

HEIRLOOM (ETHIOPIA)

SUDAN RUME

HIBRIDO DE TIMOR

ARABUSTA

SPECIES *C. ARABICA*

ROBUSTA

SPECIES *C.CANEPHORA*

SPECIES *C. LIBERICA*

RUBIACEAE FAMILY

What is a variety?

The variety is a botanical classification on a lower level than species. The *Coffea arabica* and the *Coffea canephora* are two species of coffee plant. A variety is a subgroup of individuals that display differences (in terms of their morphology, the size of the fruits, etc.) relative to the standard variety, which, in the case of the *Coffea arabica*, is the Typica variety. These different varieties come about as a result of either mutation or hybridization, depending on the case

Mutation

A mutation refers to morphological changes in a young plant relative to the standard variety (size and/or shape of plants, leaves, cherries). The mutant seedlings are considered to be a new variety if they keep their new characteristics when they produce seeds of their own.

Hybridization

A hybrid is a cross between two varieties. Hybridization can be natural or artificial.

PACAS

VILLA SARCHI

CATURRA

BOURBON ROUGE

SL 34

LAURINA (RED BOURBON)

SL 28

LIBERICA

THE CASE OF ROBUSTA

In actual fact, Robusta is not itself a species of the coffee plant, but a variety of *Coffea canephora*. How-ever, the designation *Coffea canephora* is commonly used to refer to Robusta, the reason being that Robusta is the original and most widely cultivated variety of those belonging to the *Canephora* species (the other consumable varieties being Kouillou, Conilon, Gimé, and Niaouli).

Some well-known hybrid varieties

ICATU =
((ARABICA + ROBUSTA) + MUNDO NUOVO) + CATUAI

CATIMOR =
CATURRA + HIBRIDO DE TIMOR

SARCHIMOR =
VILLA SARCHI + HIBRIDO DE TIMOR

RUIRU 11 =
SUDAN RUME + HIBRIDO DE TIMOR + SL 28 + SL 34

HIBRIDO DE TIMOR, AN EXCEPTIONAL CROSS

The *Arabusta* family is the result of a cross between the *Coffea canephora* species and the *Coffea arabica* species. The principal and most common of the hybrids in this family is Hibrido de Timor. This cross is both resilient and strong in taste, which is why Hibrido de Timor is often used in other hybrids.

SEASONALITY AND FRESHNESS OF GREEN COFFEE

It is easy to forget that coffee is a fresh, seasonal product, as it comes from far away and undergoes a raft of processes between the time the cherries are picked and the time the bags of green coffee arrive at the roasting house. However, seasonality and freshness are key factors when it comes to fully appreciating specialty coffees.

A seasonal product

Coffee is harvested either once or twice a year (one main harvest, followed by a second smaller one), depending on whether it is grown in the tropical or subtropical zone. The duration of the harvesting varies depending on the country, but it never stretches over the entire year. Hence, coffee, like any other agricultural product, is a "seasonal product." To get a better idea of the coffee seasons and help you make your choices, it is worth referring to a calendar of harvests in the various producing countries (see the calendar of harvests opposite).

NO VINTAGES

With coffees, in contrast to wines, there is no such thing as a quality vintage. But just as chefs cook with seasonal products, specialty coffee roasters also work with "coffees in season."

A matter of freshness

The freshness of the green coffee beans determines the length of time during which their sensory qualities are at their best. This period lasts several months, or a year in some cases. It is possible to prolong the life of the green bean by freezing it in a sealed vacuum bag. The downsides of this are the additional cost, and the fact that defrosted green beans age more quickly.

DATE OF HARVEST ON COFFEE PACKAGES

The roast date is often specified on coffee packages, but the year of harvest is not yet stated as standard. Do not hesitate to ask the roaster.

"Past crop" and "old crop"

"Past crop" refers to coffee beans from a past harvest. At this stage in their life cycle, the green beans are starting to decline in quality, and the coffee is likely to lose its flavor qualities. The lipids contained in the bean break down and oxidize, the moisture level (about 11 percent) varies and may fall, or even rise, if the coffee is stored under poor conditions. The coffee then develops a more noticeable woody flavor, its acidity declines, and it emits an odor resembling burlap sacks. In this case one can refer to the coffee as having an "old crop" flavor profile. The green coffee from a harvest may become "old crop" if the drying, storage in the country of origin, transport, or storage after roasting is performed in poor conditions.

Calendar of harvests

There are one or two harvest periods a year, depending on the producer country.
Information about coffee cultivation in each country can be found from page 142 onward.

	J	F	M	A	M	J	J	A	S	O	N	D
BOLIVIA							■	■	■	■		
BRAZIL					■	■						
BURUNDI			■	■								
COLOMBIA	■	■									■	■
COSTA RICA	■	■	■								■	■
EL SALVADOR	■	■	■								■	■
ECUADOR					■	■	■	■				
ETHIOPIA	■	■									■	■
GUATEMALA	■	■	■								■	■
HAWAII	■								■	■	■	
HONDURAS		■	■	■							■	■
INDIA	■	■										
INDONESIA (SULAWESI)	■	■	■	■	■					■	■	■
INDONESIA (SUMATRA)										■	■	■
JAMAICA	■	■	■						■	■		
KENYA	■	■									■	■
RÉUNION ISLAND	■	■								■	■	■
MEXICO	■	■	■								■	■
NICARAGUA	■	■	■							■	■	■
PANAMA	■	■									■	■
PERU							■	■	■			
RWANDA			■	■	■	■	■					

TRADITIONAL METHODS OF DRYING COFFEE

Once harvested, the coffee cherry, perfectly ripe, has to be dried in order to extract the beans. The drying method used has a marked impact on the coffee's flavor profile.

Harvesting of the coffee

The cherries are, for the most part, harvested by hand; the pickers harvest only the ripe, undamaged cherries (which may be red or yellow, depending on the variety), leaving any overripe or unripe (dark or green) cherries behind. As the cherries do not all ripen at the same rate, several pickings are required to ensure all cherries are picked when they are at their best. The pickers are generally paid by weight, and can collect between 110 and 265 lb of cherries a day. Another manual picking method known as "strip picking" is sometimes used, in which all the cherries on the branches of the coffee tree are stripped off at one time. The emphasis with this method is on quantity and speed. Mechanical harvesting is done by machines programmed to shake the branches of the coffee trees, causing only the ripe cherries to drop off. It is a method that works well for *Coffea arabica*, whose cherries fall off easily. But machines can only be used on plantations at low altitude and on land that is not too steep. The cherries can be stored for up to eight hours before being dried. After that, fermentation sets in and there is a risk of producing "stinky cherries."

MANUAL HARVESTING OF THE RIPE CHERRIES, LEAVING THE UNRIPE ONES FOR LATER

Drying with the dry process: Natural coffee

This traditional method of drying coffee is also known as "unwashed" or "natural coffee" (as opposed to washed coffees), as the cherries stay whole.

Where?
Regions where the dry season is well defined (Brazil, Ethiopia, Panama, Costa Rica).

How long does it take?
Between ten and thirty days.

Principle
The cherries are spread out in a layer that, ideally, should be the thickness of two cherries, on a concrete patio or, preferably, on African raised beds, and turned regularly to ensure the cherries ferment uniformly in contact with the air. At nighttime they are covered to keep them from absorbing any nocturnal moisture. The moisture level in the fresh cherries goes from 70 percent to 15–30 percent during drying, and is then reduced further to 10–12 percent (the optimum level in terms of keeping the beans fresh).

Result
Intense, fruity aromas, like an explosion in the nose and mouth. The coffee will have body, but the finish may not always be clean.

Sometimes the nose can be winey, recalling certain alcohols and, in bad cases, vinegar.

➕ Few tools required, and no need for big investments in equipment.
➖ • Picking is sometimes haphazard.
• Need space to spread out the cherries at peak harvest times.
• A lot of workers are needed, and careful monitoring is required to obtain a coffee that is as uniform as a washed coffee.

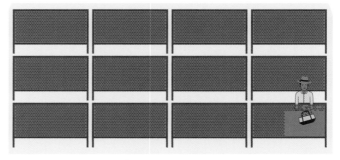

AFRICAN RAISED BEDS (MATTING RAISED UP ON TRESTLES SO THAT THE CHERRIES ARE BETTER AERATED)

Drying with the wet process: Washed coffee

The wet process was developed by Dutch coffee producers in the seventeenth century on the island of Java, where the dry process is impracticable because of the high humidity and large amount of precipitation.

Where?
In production regions with high humidity levels (Ethiopia, Kenya, Rwanda, El Salvador, Colombia, Panama).
How long does it take?
• Between 6 and 72 hours—between 12 and 36 hours on average—for the fermentation
• Between 4 and 10 days for the drying
Principle
The coffee cherries are mechanically pulped and the beans are immersed in water to remove the mucilage by means of a fermentation process. The beans are then cleaned and dried.

Result
Cleaner than a natural coffee, but also less body, and more pronounced acidity.

➕ The activity of the enzymes in the mucilage and the microorganisms that develop in the water cause the pH of the beans to fall to below 5, giving the washed coffee a more pronounced acidity.
➖ Uses a lot of water (up to 22 gallons per kilo of cherries processed), which becomes polluted with nitrates despite efforts to recycle and reduce waste.

Method

1 The cherries are immersed in a water tank: the ripe cherries, which are heavier, sink to the bottom, whereas the debris and unripe cherries float to the surface.

2 The "good" cherries are mechanically pulped; in other words, their skin and part of the pulp are removed.

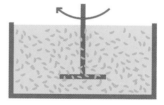

3 The coffee beans, still covered with a layer of pulp, are immersed in baths to prompt the fermentation of the mucilage. The temperature is kept at a maximum of 104°F and the beans are regularly stirred to ensure even fermentation.

4 The coffee beans are washed in sluices, and a second sorting takes place: the ripe beans sink to the bottom and the defective ones stay on the surface.

5 The beans are dried on African raised beds or in large hot-air drums until their moisture level is down to 10–12 percent.

HYBRID METHODS OF DRYING COFFEE

The following are combined methods, blending elements of the dry and wet processes described on the previous pages.

Hybrid methods

Pulped natural
This method, developed in Brazil in the 1990s, combines the selection process of the wet method and the dry fermentation of the natural coffee method.

Honey process
This is the other name by which the "pulped natural" method is known outside of Brazil and Central America. The honey process is performed to different degrees, leaving a higher or lower percentage of the mucilage still attached to the parchment around the beans. The more mucilage is left behind, the darker the color of the parchment when drying in the sun.

WHITE HONEY	YELLOW HONEY	RED HONEY	BLACK HONEY
80–90%	50–75%	5–50%	MINIMAL

HONEY PROCESSES PERFORMED TO DIFFERENT DEGREES, WITH A HIGHER OR LOWER PERCENTAGE OF THE MUCILAGE REMOVED

How long does it take?
From seven to twelve days (depending on weather conditions).

Principle
Pulpers separate the ripe, softer cherries from the unripe, harder ones by passing them through a screen. The beans, which still have mucilage attached to their parchment, are then sun-dried on African beds in a layer 1 to 2 inches thick, and are turned regularly to ensure they dry evenly.

Result
A reasonably clean coffee with more body than a washed coffee, but also less acidity. The taste in the cup is more like that of the natural coffees.

➕ • Uses little water
• Good sorting
• Consistent coffee
➖ Large capital investment required for pulping equipment

Semiwashed coffee, or *giling basah*

This method shares the same initial steps as wet processing, but drying is done in two stages.

> ### GILING BASAH
> *Giling basah* is an Indonesian term meaning "wet hulled."

Where?
Only in Indonesia, in Sumatra and Sulawesi in particular.

How long does it take?
• Fermentation in water generally takes one night.
• Five to seven days for the drying of the beans without their parchment.

Principle
The fruits have their skins removed, and are then immersed in water tanks to detach the mucilage by fermentation. The beans, now covered only in parchment, are put to dry until their moisture content has fallen to just 40 percent. The beans then have their parchment removed by friction in a wet-hulling machine, and are dried rapidly.

Result
Coffees with plenty of body, and not very pronounced acidity.
➕ A solution to the problems posed by the Indonesian weather, such as humidity, which causes the coffee trees to flower and need harvesting all year round, and which also makes drying more difficult.

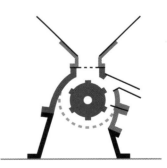

HULLING MACHINE FOR REMOVING THE PARCHMENT: WITH THEIR PARCHMENT GONE, THE BEANS DRY MORE QUICKLY.

DRYING: A RECAP

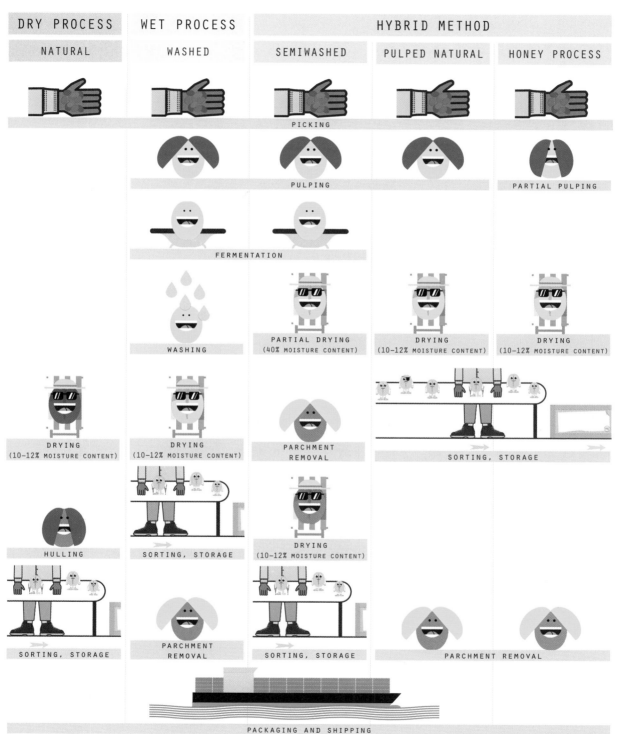

CLEANING, SORTING, AND PACKAGING OF GREEN COFFEE

The dried coffee still has to be cleaned and sorted before being packaged for shipping to the consumer countries.

Cleaning the coffee

Whatever the drying method used, the resulting dried coffee is sent to a "dry mill" to be cleaned. The aim is to get rid of all impurities (debris, stones, bits of metal, dust, leaves, etc.) by suction, followed by sieving. In the case of natural coffee and pulped natural coffee, the cherries go into a hulling machine, which crushes the dried cherries (which still have their dried skin and pulp attached) against one another and against the metal sides of the machine. The outer layers come loose and are blasted off with compressed air.

In the case of washed coffee, the machine removes the parchment (the thin membrane covering the bean). The beans are then polished to remove as much as possible of the silver skin, which is underneath the parchment (see the cross-section of the coffee bean on page 126).

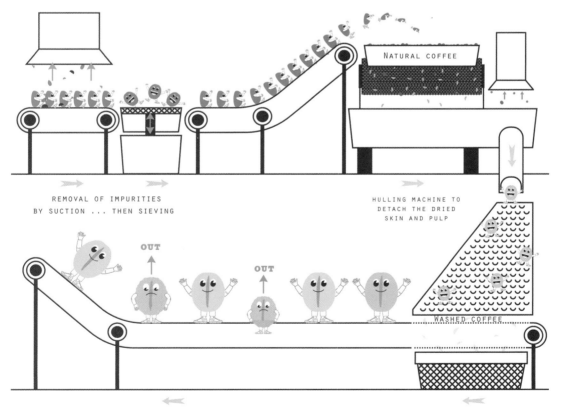

NATURAL COFFEE

REMOVAL OF IMPURITIES
BY SUCTION ... THEN SIEVING

HULLING MACHINE TO
DETACH THE DRIED
SKIN AND PULP

OUT

OUT

WASHED COFFEE

REMOVAL OF SILVER SKIN

REMOVAL OF PARCHMENT

Sorting the beans

The cleaned beans are then sorted according to certain criteria: size, density, and color:

WHAT ABOUT DEFECTIVE BEANS?

The beans rejected during sorting do not end up in the trash! There is a market for poor-quality beans, referred to as "broken beans" (for industrial espresso, instant-coffee blends, etc.), so low-grade batches get traded on the commodity market.

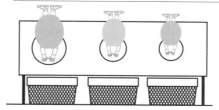

STEP 1
Mechanical or manual separation of the dense (good-quality) beans from the light (poor-quality) beans.

STEP 2
Size-sorting of the beans by means of screens with holes of different sizes.

STEP 3
Selection of beans by color on conveyor belts equipped with color detectors:
• Black or very dark = fermented beans
• Pale, white = unripe beans
When a bean is identified as defective, it is blasted aside by a jet of air.

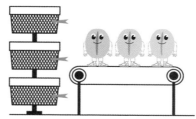

STEP 4
Final color sorting of the beans. This final manual job is performed by women sitting at conveyor belts.

Packaging

Once sorted, the coffee is bagged and ready for export. Various kinds of containers are used:

Jute bags
Traditionally, the coffee is packed in 130- to 150-lb bags. They are economical, tough, and durable, and provide good protection. Decorated with lovely designs, they are part of coffee folklore.

Vacuum packs
These appeared on the scene a few years ago, and are used primarily for batches of particularly fine coffees that sell for premium prices. The bags are then placed in boxes. They generally hold 44 to 77 lb, but some importers use boxed bags holding less than 22 lb for certain micro-batches.

GrainPro bags
A multilayer plastic bag designed to increase the shelf life of dried beans, cereal, and seeds. They preserve the flavor potential of the green coffee for longer.

COFFEE-PRODUCING COUNTRIES

The map shows all the coffee-producing countries in the world, with the rankings of the top ten.

HAWAII (UNITED STATES)

MEXICO

HONDURAS — 8

GUATEMALA — 10

EL SALVADOR

NICARAGUA

COSTA RICA

7

PANAMA

CUBA

JAMAICA

HAITI

DOMINICAN REPUBLIC

PUERTO RICO

GUADELOUPE

VENEZUELA

TRINIDAD AND TOBAGO

SURINAME

COLOMBIA

ECUADOR

PERU

3

BOLIVIA

1
BRAZIL

PARAGUAY

SIERRA LEONE
IVORY COAST

GHANA
TOGO

BENIN
NIGERIA

CAMEROON

EQUATORIAL GUINEA

GABON
CONGO

DEM. REP. OF CONGO

ANGOLA

ARABICA
PRODUCERS

ROBUSTA
PRODUCERS

ARABIC AND ROBUSTA
PRODUCERS

NEPAL

6

BURMA

YEMEN
SUDAN
CENTRAL
AFRICAN REP.
ETHIOPIA
KENYA

5

9

UGANDA
RWANDA
BURUNDI
TANZANIA
ZAMBIA
MOZAMBIQUE

INDIA

SRI LANKA

LAOS
THAILAND
CAMBODIA

CHINA

VIETNAM

PHILIPPINES

2

MALAYSIA

PAPUA NEW GUINEA

4

INDONESIA

AUSTRALIA

MADAGASCAR

RÉUNION
ISLAND

MALAWI
ZIMBABWE

SOUTH AFRICA

International Coffee Organization figures for 2014

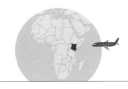

ETHIOPIA

Ethiopia is known as the birthplace of coffee. Here, unlike in many other producer countries, coffee cultivation is not a legacy of colonization: the coffee plant used to grow wild or semi-wild here, in a region where much of the land lies at an altitude of over 5,000 ft.

There are few plantations and large farms; coffee is grown in gardens, in forest or semi-forest, without the use of chemicals. Ninety percent of all the coffee produced, which can be regarded as organic although not certified as such, comes from more than 700,000 small producers. Productivity is not high, and traceability stops (with the odd exception) at the washing stations, where the harvests are pooled.

In particular, Ethiopia possesses the greatest genetic diversity of coffee plants and Arabica varieties in the world, and its forests are home to the quality coffees of the future.

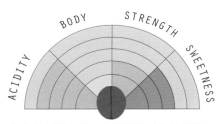

The flavors of an Ethiopian coffee:
YIRGACHEFFE ARICHA

COFFEE FACTS

▶ Annual production: 438,168 US tons

▶ World market share: 4.6%

▶ Producer's world ranking: 5th

▶ Principal varieties: old varieties

▶ Harvest period(s): November–February

▶ Drying: wet process and dry process

▶ Cup characteristics:

• Wet-processed coffees → floral, citric acidity, and light body
• Dry-processed coffees → notes of tropical fruits, strawberries

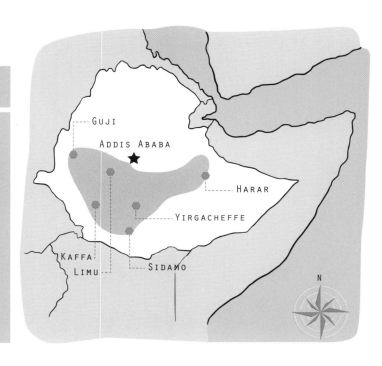

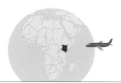

KENYA

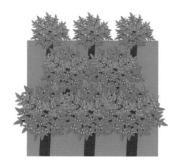

Coffee was introduced to Kenya by Westerners toward the end of the nineteenth century. It produces predominantly Arabica, particularly the SL 28, SL 34, K7, and Ruiru 11 varieties, which are wet-processed. Just over half of Kenyan coffee comes from small producers grouped by washing station, with six hundred to one thousand members per "factory," and these factories are in turn part of cooperatives. The red clay soil found in central Kenya contributes to the characteristic flavor profile. Kenya has its own bean classification, or grading system, based on bean size. Beans are sorted by passing them through screens containing holes of different diameters:

- AA: Beans with screen size 18, a diameter of over 7.22 mm. They are the most expensive lots because, in general, they give a brew of highest quality and greatest complexity.
- AB: Beans size of 16 (6.8 mm) and 15 (6.2 mm).
- PB: Peaberry (or caracole; see page 126).

These are the three reference grades used for specialty coffees.

- C, TT, T: Low-grade beans. Most of these lots are sold at auction.

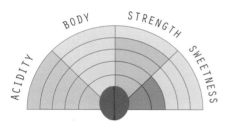

THE FLAVORS OF A KENYAN COFFEE:
GICHATHAINI AA

COFFEE FACTS

▶ Annual production: 56,217 US tons

▶ World market share: 0.6%

▶ Producer's world ranking: 16th

▶ Principal varieties: SL 28, SL 34, K7, Ruiru 11

▶ Harvest period(s): November–February

▶ Drying: wet process

▶ Characteristics: notes of red fruits and vibrant acidity

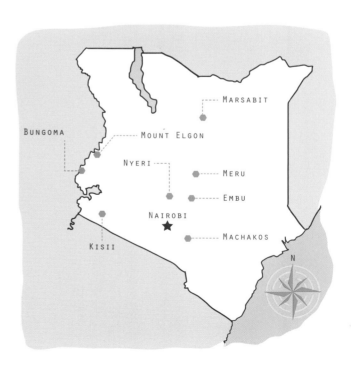

RWANDA

Coffee was brought to Rwanda in 1904 by German missionaries. The climate (regular, stable precipitation) and geology of the country (altitude of 5,000 to 6,500 ft. fertile, volcanic soils) are conducive to the cultivation of quality coffee.

Rwandan producers tend to be grouped into cooperatives, which have set up their own washing stations. Thanks to its strategy of producing specialty coffee, Rwanda commands high, stable prices. It was also the first producer country in Africa to stage a Cup of Excellence competition, in 2008.

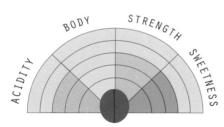

THE FLAVORS OF A RWANDAN COFFEE:
EPIPHANY MUHIRWA

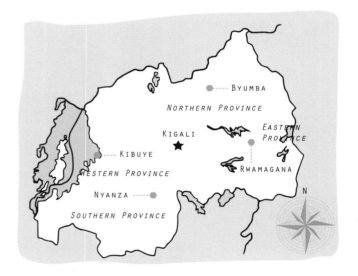

COFFEE FACTS

▶ Annual production: 18,518 US tons (99% Arabica / 1% Robusta)

▶ World market share: 0.2%

▶ Producer's world ranking: 28th

▶ Principal variety: Red Bourbon

▶ Harvest period(s): March–July

▶ Drying: wet process

▶ Coffee characteristics: floral, fruity, good acidity

THE POTATO DEFECT

In Rwanda and Burundi, coffee is sometimes affected by a bacterium that is hard to detect and which gives the ground beans an odor of old potatoes. This bacterium strikes randomly, contaminating one bean while sparing the rest of the lot. Although beans affected by this do not pose a health risk, this very unpleasant problem represents a real challenge for these two producing countries.

BURUNDI

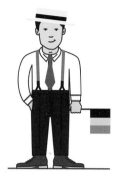

It was not until the 1930s that coffee was brought to Burundi by the Belgians. Burundi has much in common with its neighbor Rwanda: climate, soils, and altitude well-suited to coffee growing, but also the potato defect.

Burundian coffee is grown by small producers who bring their harvest to washing stations run by the SOGESTAL cooperatives. Prior to 2008, the different lots were processed together and blended. Since that date, the washing stations have been permitted to keep the lots separate, which makes for better traceability and allows the lots to be graded according to their taste quality. Burundi was the second African nation to stage a Cup of Excellence competition.

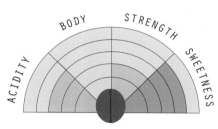

THE FLAVORS OF A BURUNDIAN COFFEE:
GICHATHAINI AA

COFFEE FACTS

▶ Annual production: 17,857 US tons

▶ World market share: 0.2%

▶ Producer's world ranking: 29th

▶ Principal variety: Red Bourbon (see page 162)

▶ Harvest period(s): March–July

▶ Drying: wet process

▶ Coffee characteristics: fruity, citric acidity

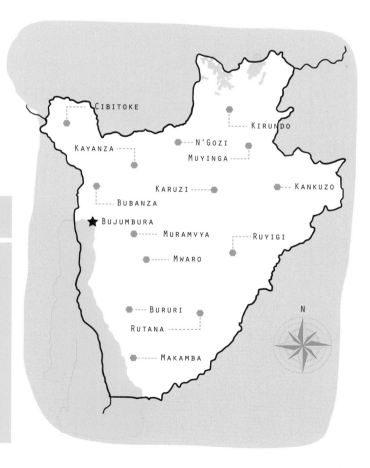

RÉUNION ISLAND

Coffee was introduced to the island in 1715. Réunion Island, which at the time was called Bourbon Island, gave its name to the first variety of coffee to be cultivated there. The Bourbon variety, itself originally from Yemen, is a variety of Typica which has undergone a natural mutation. Coffee cultivation began in the 1720s, enjoying a golden age around 1800, when the island's output reached 4,400 US tons. Then natural disasters and sugarcane farming brought about a marked drop in coffee production on Réunion. In 1771, a variety specific to the island appeared: Bourbon Pointu. After virtually dying out, it began to be cultivated again in the early 2000s. Production of this variety is very small and aimed at a niche market.

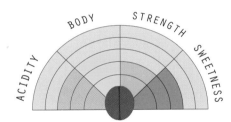

THE FLAVORS OF A RÉUNION ISLAND COFFEE:
BOURBON POINTU

COFFEE FACTS

► Annual production: 3.3 US tons

► World market share: < 0.01%

► Producer's world ranking: not ranked (niche market)

► Principal varieties: Bourbon (see page 162), Bourbon Pointu (see page 149)

► Harvest period(s): October–February

► Drying: wet process

► Characteristics: medium body, medium acidity, balanced brew

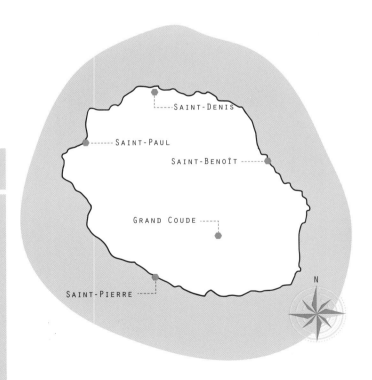

COFFEE VARIETIES

SL 28

- **Origin:** Created by Scott Laboratory in 1931, this variety is related to Bourbon and to Ethiopian varieties.
- **Plant:** large leaves and fairly large beans
- **Resistance:** good disease-resistance
- **Yield:** low
- **Recommended brewing method:** slow methods
- **Cup:** pronounced acidity and notes of red fruits

SL 34

- **Origin:** the result of a Bourbon mutation that occurred in Loresho plantation in Kabete (central Kenya)
- **Plant:** large leaves and fairly large beans
- **Yield:** high
- **Resistance:** copes well with precipitation at high altitude
- **Recommended brewing method:** slow methods
- **Cup:** recognized for its sensory qualities

BOURBON POINTU

- **Origin:** A natural mutation of the Bourbon variety, Bourbon Pointu, also known as Laurina or *Coffea arabica var. laurina*, is thought to have appeared on Réunion Island in 1771. Virtually eradicated following an epidemic in 1880, the variety was rediscovered in the early 2000s by Yoshiaki Kawashima. And, with the help of the CIRAD research organization, production was resumed.
- **Other producing country:** Madagascar
- **Plant:** small size, pyramid shaped, with small leaves and cherries. The beans are a very distinctive rectangular shape.

- **Resistance:** good drought resistance, but susceptible to leaf rust
- **Yield:** low
- **Recommended brewing method:** espresso
- **Cup:** lower level of caffeine than the other varieties of *Coffea arabica* (0.6%)

HEIRLOOM

This term is used to refer to the oldest coffee varieties.

It is used only in Ethiopia, where coffee was not imported by man. It grows naturally, and it is not easy to identify all the varieties that comprise a harvest. As a result, green coffee buyers and roasters alike use the term "heirloom" when referring to the ancient varieties of coffee from Ethiopia.

BRAZIL

300,000 FARMS

THE FLAVORS OF A BRAZILIAN COFFEE:
CAPIM BRANCO

Coffee was introduced to Brazil by the Portuguese in the eighteenth century. Brazil was soon the number one coffee-producing country in the world, and by the 1920s was already responsible for 80 percent of the coffee produced worldwide. The country is still the leading producer today, although its production share has diminished somewhat as other countries' coffee output has grown. Brazil's coffee-growing areas are for the most part located in the southeast of the country. The country's size, climate, topography (a flat country with gentle hill slopes, which, importantly, makes it possible to employ machinery), and altitude have enabled it to develop intensive coffee-farming operations. It has nearly 300,000 coffee farms, including vast estates using modern industrial methods that improve productivity and profitability, but also organic and even biodynamic farms that use fewer chemicals and endeavor to promote biodiversity on their plantations. It is possible to trace very good Brazilian coffee lots all the way to the individual plantation. It was in Brazil that the Cup of Excellence was instituted in 1999.

COFFEE FACTS

▶ Annual production: 2,998,859 US tons (67% Arabica, 33% Robusta)

▶ World market share: 32%

▶ Producer's world ranking: 1st

▶ Principal varieties: Mundo Novo, Caturra (see page 163), Icatu, Bourbon (see page 162), Catuai (see page 162)

▶ Harvest period(s): May–August

▶ Drying: dry process and wet process

▶ Characteristics: Brazilian coffees are renowned for their very low acidity, sweetness, and nutty overtones; this is why they are used as the base for numerous blends.

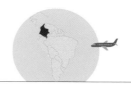

COLOMBIA

100% Colombian Coffee

Coffee was brought to Colombia at the end of the eighteenth century and commercial production began in the early nineteenth century. There are almost 500,000 farms (most of them small in size) producing coffee in Colombia. The Andes mountain range generates numerous microclimates conducive to coffee cultivation, but the topography of the country prevents any expansion of production. In many cases the very steep mountain slopes prevent the use of any machinery whatsoever, and because there are few trees, the soil in these steep terrains is vulnerable to erosion. So producers tend to focus on the quality of their output. Only Arabica varieties are cultivated. In 1960, the New York advertising agency Doyle Dane Bernbach (now know as DDB Worldwide) invented the figure of Juan Valdez, the fictional character on the "Colombian Coffee" quality label. This romantic image of the humble coffee producer with his mule did much to enhance Colombian coffee's reputation for quality. Nowadays coffee only accounts for 10 percent of the country's exports, but it remains a strong marker of national identity.

THE FLAVORS OF A COLOMBIAN COFFEE:
LA VIRGINIA, HUILA

COFFEE FACTS

▶ Annual production: 826,733 US tons

▶ World market share: 8.8%

▶ Producer's world ranking: 3rd

▶ Principal varieties: Caturra, Castillo

▶ Harvest periods: all year round on account of the many different microclimates

▶ Drying: wet process

▶ Characteristics: body, sweetness, medium acidity

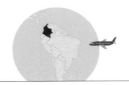

ECUADOR

Coffee was introduced to Ecuador in 1860, and was first cultivated in the Manabi region. Coffee production peaked in the 1980s, before declining in the 1990s as a result of a major economic recession. A large proportion of Ecuador's coffee output goes into making instant coffee, therefore priority is given to Robusta, and to high-yield but low-quality Arabica. However, there is real scope for the cultivation of quality coffee in Ecuador, especially at high altitude. To address this challenge, the country needs to select varieties known for their brew quality (Typica, Bourbon), and to counteract the high cost of labor.

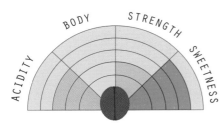

THE FLAVORS OF AN ECUADORIAN COFFEE: LAS TOLAS

COFFEE FACTS

▶ Annual production: 42,990 US tons (60% Arabica, 40% Robusta)

▶ World market share: 0.45%

▶ Producer's world ranking: 20th

▶ Principal varieties: Typica, Bourbon, Caturra

▶ Harvest period(s): May–September

▶ Drying: wet process and dry process

▶ Characteristics: good acidity, balanced brew

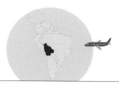

BOLIVIA

Coffee is thought to have arrived in Bolivia in the nineteenth century. Its favorable climate (clearly demarcated dry and wet seasons) and ideal altitude mean it has good potential for coffee cultivation. However, the country's lack of facilities and landlocked situation, which mean exports have to go via Peru, are holding back its development. Output is very modest. Most of the approximately 23,000 farms are family-run, covering an area of 5 to 20 acres. Coffee from Bolivia is organic, albeit uncertified, as, on the whole, producers cannot afford to buy chemicals. Bolivian coffee offers good traceability; the origin of a specific lot can be traced right back to the farm. There are some excellent Bolivian coffees.

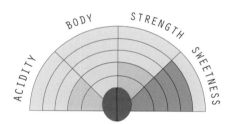

THE FLAVORS OF A BOLIVIAN COFFEE:
7 ESTRELLAS

COFFEE FACTS

▶ Annual production: 7,936 US tons

▶ World market share: 0.08%

▶ Producer's world ranking: 33rd

▶ Principal varieties: Typica and Caturra

▶ Harvest period(s): July–October

▶ Drying: wet process

▶ Characteristics: Bolivian coffee does not have a genuinely distinctive flavor profile. It can be sweet and well rounded, with low acidity.

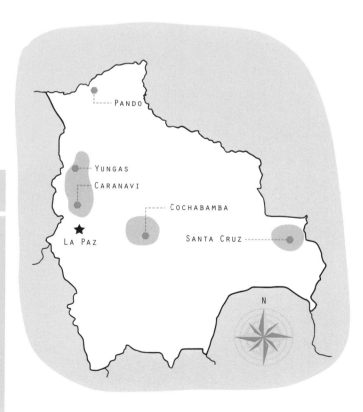

PERU

Coffee appeared in Peru in the eigthteenth century, and started to be exported in the nineteenth century. Peru has become the world's leading producer of organic and even fair trade coffee by volume. One hundred twenty thousand farms of less than 7 acres each produce the vast majority of Peruvian coffee. Some of the plantations are situated at very high altitude (7,200 ft). Overshadowed by the two large producing countries of South America—Brazil and Colombia—Peruvian coffee (like Bolivian) suffers from a lack of identity.

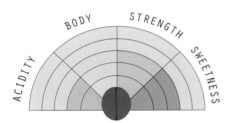

THE FLAVORS OF A PERUVIAN COFFEE:
EL MANGO

COFFEE FACTS

▶ Annual production: 224,871 US tons

▶ World market share: 2.4%

▶ Producer's world ranking: 11th

▶ Principal varieties grown: Typica, Bourbon, Caturra

▶ Harvest period(s): July–September

▶ Drying: wet process

▶ Characteristics: sweet, clean, lacks complexity

Coffee varieties

MUNDO NOVO

- **Origin:** This natural hybrid (*Sumatra x bourbon*) was discovered in Brazil in the 1940s.
- **Plant:** large with red cherries
- **Resistance:** good disease resistance at medium to high altitude
- **Yield:** high (30% higher than Bourbon)
- **Recommended brewing method:** espresso
- **Cup:** Prized for its characteristics in Brazil, but it is sometimes lacking in sweetness.

ICATU

- **Origin:** This hybrid ([*Arabica x C. canephora*] *x mundo novo x catuai*) is said to have been created in Brazil in 1985, but was not officially recognized until 1993.
- **Plant:** large with large cherries; needs to be grown above 2,600 ft of altitude
- **Resistance:** resistant to diseases, and particularly to leaf rust (see page 131)
- **Yield:** 30–50% higher than Mundo Novo
- **Recommended brewing method:** espresso
- **Cup:** Reputed to be of moderate quality due to the Robusta genes. However, it can yield a remarkably good brew when cultivated well.

TYPICA

- **Origin:** Typica is the oldest cultivar of Arabica. It has given rise, by hybridization, to several varieties of Arabica, such as Blue Mountain and Maragogype.
- **Other coffee-producing countries:** The overwhelming majority of coffee-producing countries grow Typica, even in small quantities.
- **Plant:** quite large, conical in shape, grows to a height of 11–20 ft with copper-colored leaves
- **Resistance:** better at high altitude
- **Yield:** relatively low
- **Recommended brewing method:** espresso and slow methods
- **Cup:** It is recognized for its flavor complexity.

COSTA RICA

It was in the eighteenth century that the first coffee shrubs were planted in Costa Rica, and in 1832 the country started exporting to Europe. Nowadays, it is home to around fifty thousand producers with farms of less than 12 acres, growing only Arabica varieties; Robusta production is prohibited by law. In the 2000s, to respond to market demand for specialty coffee, numerous microstations were set up, enabling small-scale producers to process their harvest separately and independently. Lots from different farms, which until then had all been processed together, are now traceable.

The growers, having taken control of their production in this way, have been able to experiment and branch out in terms of their drying methods. What's more, these stations employ creative approaches to ensure the impact of coffee production on nature is reduced and environmental legislation complied with. This Costa Rican infrastructure is ideal for the development of quality coffee.

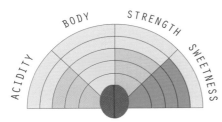

THE FLAVORS OF A COSTA RICAN COFFEE:
HACIENDA VALERIO

COFFEE FACTS

▶ Annual production: 99,737 US tons

▶ World market share: 1%

▶ Producer's world ranking: 14th

▶ Principal varieties: Caturra, Villa Sarchi, Catuai

▶ Harvest period: November–March

▶ Drying: honey, dry process, wet process

▶ Characteristics: sweetness, good acidity, and complex texture

PANAMA

Coffee cultivation began in Panama at the end of the nineteenth century. The rich volcanic soil, high altitude, and high humidity are all conducive to coffee growing. In addition, multiple microclimates coexist within a relatively limited production area. The coffee is produced on family farms or medium-sized plantations. After the coffee crisis in 1996, the Panamanian coffee industry decided to focus on specialty coffee to boost growth. Today, despite its modest output, Panama is a respected player in this market, due in particular to the production of Geisha, a variety with strong taste potential that thrives in this terrain. The best lots are sold at online auctions. Traceability is excellent. These lots can be traced right back to their individual plot on the farm where they were grown.

THE FLAVORS OF A PANAMANIAN COFFEE:
GEISHA

COFFEE FACTS

▶ Annual production: 628 US tons

▶ World market share: 0.07%

▶ Producer's world ranking: 36th

▶ Principal varieties: Geisha, Caturra, Typica, Bourbon, Catuai

▶ Harvest period: November–March

▶ Drying: wet process, dry process

▶ Characteristics of very good Geishas: sweet, elegant, balanced, complex, light-bodied, floral, and citrusy

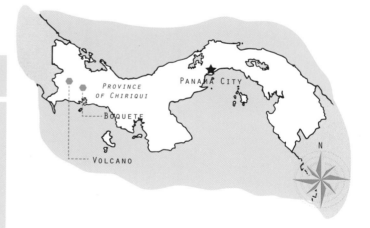

GUATEMALA

Coffee is said to have been introduced to Guatemala by Jesuits in the mid-eighteenth century. The first exports to Europe date back to 1859. The country has a varied topography, with mountains, volcanic soils, plains, and numerous microclimates, which help produce coffees with distinct and very varied flavor profiles. These days, coffee accounts for a large share of the country's agricultural exports. There are approximately 125,000 producers growing coffee across an area of 667,184 acres in several parts of the country. Microstations have sprung up around the country, making it possible to produce microlots with guaranteed traceability. So more and more producers are setting up their own washing stations, enabling them to control this crucial stage.

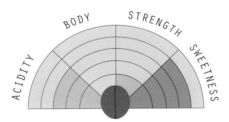

THE FLAVORS OF A GUATEMALAN COFFEE:
FINCA EL PILAR

COFFEE FACTS

▶ Annual production: 231,485 US tons (99.6% Arabica, 0.4% Robusta)

▶ World market share: 2.5%

▶ Producer's world ranking: 10th

▶ Principal varieties: Bourbon (see page 162), Catuai, Maragogype (see page 167)

▶ Harvest period: November–March

▶ Drying: wet process

▶ Characteristics: very varied flavor profiles depending on the terroir: for example, sweetness, body, roundness with chocolaty to floral notes, tanginess

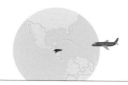

HONDURAS

The first coffee plants are thought to have been planted in Honduras at the end of the eighteenth century. Today, the country has become a major coffee producer, with more than 100,000 families involved in coffee growing, predominantly on small plantations. Although its environmental conditions are similar to those in other Central American countries, transport and infrastructure development for the processing of coffee cherries remains a real challenge for Honduras. In some areas the very humid climate makes drying on drying patios difficult. To counter this problem, producers either use tunnels, or a combination of sun-drying and mechanical drying. For many years, Honduran coffee, which is of low quality, was destined for the commodity market. Recently the Honduran Coffee Institute (IHCAFE) has started providing technical, practical, and educational assistance to small producers with a view to improving the quality of their output.

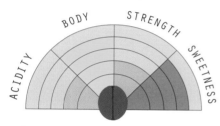

THE FLAVORS OF A HONDURAN COFFEE:
JESUS MORENO

COFFEE FACTS

▶ Annual production: 357,148 US tons
▶ World market share: 3.8%
▶ Producer's world ranking: 7th
▶ Principal varieties: Caturra, Catuai, Pacas, Typica
▶ Harvest period: November–April
▶ Drying: wet process
▶ Characteristics: Honduran coffees can be both sweet and light, and complex and fruity with a vibrant acidity.

EL SALVADOR

It was back in the nineteenth century that the first coffee plants were introduced to El Salvador. Originally, production was intended for national consumption; then, in around 1880, the government started encouraging producers to export their coffee. Nowadays, a total of around twenty thousand growers with medium-sized plantations produce coffee that has a reputation for quality. Bourbon accounts for more than 60 percent, and it is this, growers believe, that gives Salvadorian coffee its distinctive character. Pacas and Pacamara are also cultivated there. The large majority of the coffees are grown under shade, which plays an important part in combating deforestation and soil erosion. Infrastructure and traceability are good. The Salvadorian Coffee Institute (Consejo Salvadoreño del Café) also plays an instrumental role in promoting national coffee production and spreading the word above all about the quality of the terroir, with its rich volcanic soil, and the Bourbon cultivar that has been grown there ever since coffee was introduced to El Salvador in the nineteenth century

THE FLAVORS OF A SALVADORIAN COFFEE:
FINCA LA FANY

COFFEE FACTS

▶ Annual production: 44,974 US tons

▶ World market share: 0.48%

▶ Producer's world ranking: 18th

▶ Principal varieties: Bourbon, Pacas, Pacamara (see page 163)

▶ Harvest period: November–March

▶ Drying: wet process, dry process

▶ Characteristics: plenty of body, creamy, mild acidity, balanced

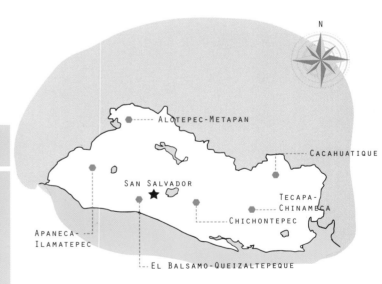

NICARAGUA

Nicaragua has been producing coffee since the mid-nineteenth century. Although it accounts for the largest share of the country's exports, this coffee is little known due to the country's long periods of political instability, financial crises, and natural disasters. Generally speaking, the average farm size is 7 acres. Until recently, traceability was poor, as the harvests of different producers were pooled at large washing stations. Now some producers have recognized the advantage of focusing on the quality of the coffee and on lot traceability. Things are starting to change.

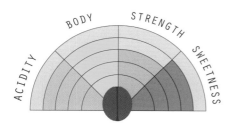

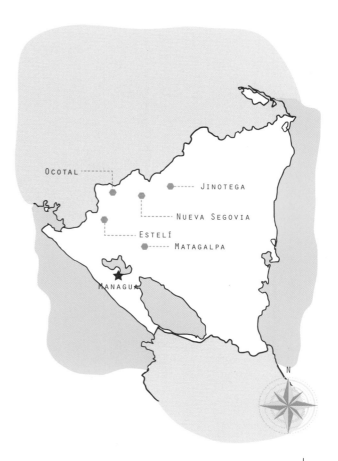

COFFEE FACTS

▶ Annual production: 132,277 US tons

▶ World market share: 1.4%

▶ Producer's world ranking: 13th

▶ Principal varieties: Caturra, Pacamara, Bourbon, Maragogype, Catuai, Catimor

▶ Harvest period: October–March

▶ Drying: wet process, dry process, pulped natural (see page 138)

▶ Characteristics: profiles ranging from sweet with chocolaty notes to floral and tangy

Coffee varieties

CATUAI

- **Origin:** This hybrid (*mundo novo x caturra jaune*) originating from Brazil came onto the market in 1968.
- **Other producer countries:** widely cultivated in Brazil and Central America
- **Plant:** small shrub
- **Resistance:** Copes well with wind and bad weather (the cherries do not drop off easily). Catuai is a high-yielding variety that grows best at 2,600 ft and above.
- **Yield:** high
- **Recommended brewing method:** espresso
- **Cup:** standard quality

BOURBON

- **Origin:** Bourbon is a natural mutation of Typica originally found on Réunion Island (which, prior to the French revolution, was called Bourbon Island). It comes in several varieties that produce different-colored cherries (red, yellow, and orange).
- **Other producer countries:** The great majority of coffee-growing countries produce Bourbon.
- **Plant:** Bourbon cherries are smaller than Typica cherries.
- **Yield:** Although its yield is 20–30 percent higher than Typica, Bourbon is regarded as a low-yielding variety.
- **Resistance:** better at altitudes of between 3,200 and 6,500 ft
- **Recommended brewing method:** espresso for Red Bourbon/slow methods and in iced coffee for Yellow Bourbon
- **Cup:** fine, light body, sweet

GEISHA

- **Origin:** This variety is thought to have originated close to a town called Gesha in southwest Ethiopia, where it was discovered in 1931. In 1932, Gesha beans were introduced to Kenya. In the 1950s, there were attempts to cultivate Gesha in Costa Rica, but it was not until 1963 that this variety was introduced in Panama. In the 2000s, the variety, rechristened Geisha, captured the attention of the specialty coffee sector.
- **Other producer countries:** Colombia and Costa Rica
- **Plant:** tall, with long leaves, cherries, and beans
- **Resistance:** quite good
- **Yield:** low, with better results at altitudes of over 5,000 ft, and only in certain soils
- **Recommended brewing method:** Slow methods are preferable.
- **Cup:** Very distinctive flavor profile, floral, very refined, complex, with the body of a tea and aromas of citrus fruits and berries. Geisha has been crowned the winner in several contests to find the best coffees in Panama.

PACAS

- **Origin:** Developed as a mutation of Bourbon. This variety was discovered in 1949 in El Salvador by a Salvadorian grower by the name of Pacas.
- **Plant:** smaller than the Bourbon plant
- **Resistance:** better disease resistance than Bourbon
- **Yield:** quite good at high altitude
- **Recommended brewing method:** espresso
- **Cup:** fairly similar to Bourbon

PACAMARA

- **Origin:** This hybrid (*pacas x maragogype*) was created in El Salvador in 1958, the fruit of a partnership between France and CIRAD. The aim was to combine certain characteristics of Pacas with those of Maragogype.
- **Other producer countries:** Mexico, Nicaragua, Colombia, Honduras, and Guatemala
- **Plant:** small, but produces large beans
- **Resistance:** Copes well with wind and bad weather. A robust plant.
- **Yield:** better than Pacas
- **Recommended brewing method:** slow methods
- **Cup:** flavor profile sometimes complex with good acidity when cultivated in good conditions at high altitude

VILLALOBOS

- **Origin:** mutation of Costa Rican Bourbon
- **Plant:** normal size cherries
- **Resistance:** wind-resistant
- **Yield:** high at high altitude
- **Recommended brewing method:** espresso and filter
- **Cup:** beans with good sensory qualities

CATURRA

- **Origin:** This mutation of Bourbon was discovered in Brazil close to the town of Caturra in 1937.
- **Producer countries:** Costa Rica and Nicaragua. Not widely grown in Brazil.
- **Plant:** small shrub with large leaves
- **Resistance:** better than that of Bourbon or Typica
- **Yield:** good, higher than Bourbon
- **Recommended brewing method:** espresso and slow methods
- Cup: Highly regarded in Colombia. Generally, the quality in the cup is not as good as Bourbon.

VILLA SARCHI

- **Origin:** natural mutation of Bourbon found near the town of Sarchi (Costa Rica)
- **Plant:** normal-size cherries, bronze-colored leaves
- **Resistance:** quite low
- **Yield:** productive at high altitude
- **Recommended brewing method:** espresso
- **Cup:** acidity and sweetness, clean

MEXICO

Coffee was introduced to Mexico via the Antilles in the late eighteenth century. Records show the first coffee was exported in 1802.

Mexican coffee was long regarded as inexpensive but of little interest. Producers had to contend with limited yields, an inadequate infrastructure, and meager support from the authorities. In 2012, things started to change when Mexico held its own Cup of Excellence competition, which gave Mexican producers an opportunity to showcase distinctive, high-quality coffees. Today, Mexico, with its medium-sized plantations, has become a major coffee producer, especially of coffees certified fair trade and organic.

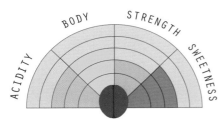

THE FLAVORS OF A MEXICAN COFFEE:
FINCA KASSANDRA

COFFEE FACTS

▶ Annual production: 257,940 US tons

▶ World market share: 2.75%

▶ Producer's world ranking: 8th

▶ Principal varieties: Maragogype, Pacamara, Bourbon, Typica, Caturra, Mundo Novo, Catuai, Catimor

▶ Harvest period: November–March

▶ Drying: wet process

▶ Characteristics: sweetness, lightness; but well-rounded, balanced coffees with a malic and citric acidity also feature

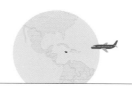

JAMAICA

In 1728, the governor of Jamaica, Sir Nicholas Lawes, obtained seeds from coffee trees from Martinique. Coffee was first grown in the area around Kingston, before spreading to the slopes of the Blue Mountain region, which gave its name to Jamaica's iconic coffee variety. Blue Mountain, which has long been one of the most expensive coffees in the world, is unique in that it is exported in barrels, rather than the traditional jute bags. Virtually all of the output is consumed in Japan and the United States. The famed Blue Mountain coffee is held in high esteem and has a reputation as a top-of-the-line, premium coffee, but is perhaps a little overrated compared to other specialty coffees.

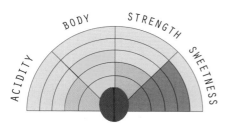

THE FLAVORS OF A JAMAICAN COFFEE:
BLUE MOUNTAIN

COFFEE FACTS

▶ Annual production: 1,102 US tons

▶ World market share: less than 0.1%

▶ Producer's world ranking: 44th

▶ Principal varieties: Blue Mountain, Bourbon, Typica

▶ Harvest period: September–March

▶ Drying: wet process

▶ Characteristics: sweet, rich, syrupy

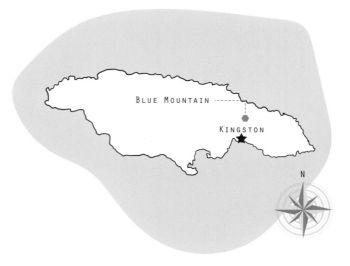

HAWAII

The first coffee plants were brought to Hawaii from Brazil in 1825. Production remained modest until the 1980s, with growers preferring to cultivate sugarcane. The most highly reputed Hawaiian coffee comes from Kona, on the main island of the archipelago. Coffees bearing the Kona label must include at least 10 percent Kona-grown coffee. Hawaiian coffee is fairly expensive, owing to the higher cost of labor and production costs than in other producing countries.

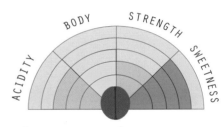

THE FLAVORS OF A HAWAIIAN COFFEE:
KONA EXTRA FANCY

COFFEE FACTS

▶ Annual production: 3,858 US tons

▶ World market share: less than 0.1%

▶ Producer's world ranking: 41st

▶ Principal varieties: Typica, Catuai

▶ Harvest period: September–January

▶ Drying: wet process and dry process

▶ Characteristics: medium body, low acidity

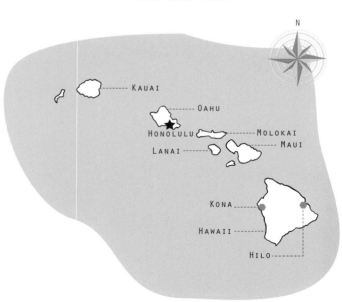

COFFEE VARIETIES

BLUE MOUNTAIN

- **Origin:** Variety derived from Typica and other varieties. It is named after the Blue Mountain coffee region of Jamaica.
- **Other producer countries:** Kona (Hawaii) and western Kenya since 1913
- **Plant:** like Typica, quite tall, conical in shape, grows to a height of 11 to 20 ft, with copper-colored leaves
- **Resistance:** fairly resilient and able to cope with high altitude

- **Yield:** low
- **Recommended brewing method:** espresso and filter
- **Cup:** well rounded

MARAGOGYPE

- **Origin:** This natural mutation of Typica was discovered in the Maragogype region in the state of Bahia, Brazil.
- **Producer countries:** Guatemala and Brazil
- **Plant:** very tall, with large leaves, large cherries, and large seeds
- **Resistance:** nothing of note

- **Yield:** low
- **Recommended brewing method:** espresso and filter
- **Cup:** sweet and fruity

KENT

- **Origin:** A mutation of Typica that originated in India. This variety has been widely grown in India since the 1930s. It served as a base for the K7 variety grown in Kenya.
- **Producer countries:** India and Tanzania
- **Plant:** like Typica, but the seeds are larger
- **Resistance:** relatively good resistance to leaf rust

- **Yield:** high
- **Recommended brewing method:** espresso
- **Cup:** light acidity and roundness

INDONESIA

Indonesia started exporting coffee to Europe in 1711 via the Dutch East India Company. At that time only Arabica varieties were cultivated, but in 1876, much of the harvest was wiped out by a leaf rust epidemic. The producers then switched to growing Robusta, which has much better resistance to this fungal disease. Nowadays, the large majority of the coffee produced in Indonesia is Robusta. Ninety percent of the coffee plantations in the archipelago are extremely small in size (2 to 5 acres). The most commonly cultivated varieties are Typica, Hibrido de Timor (commonly known as "Tim" in Sumatra), Caturra, and Catimor.

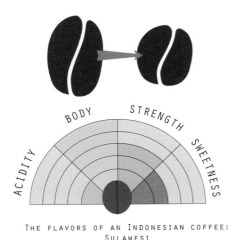

ACIDITY — BODY — STRENGTH — SWEETNESS

THE FLAVORS OF AN INDONESIAN COFFEE:
SULAWESI

COFFEE FACTS

▶ Annual production: 595,248 US tons (16.5% Arabica, 83.5% Robusta)

▶ World market share: 6.3%

▶ Producer's world ranking: 4th

▶ Principal varieties: Typica (see page 155), Hibrido de Timor, Caturra (see page 163), Catimor

▶ Harvest periods: October–May (Sulawesi), October–March (Sumatra), June–October (Java)

▶ Drying: semiwashed (*giling basah*), dry process, wet process

▶ Characteristics:
• Sumatran coffees are characterized by notes of wood and spice, plenty of body, and very low acidity.
• The coffees of Sulawesi have low acidity, a rich texture, and notes of herbs and spices.
• Javan coffees are noted for their body, low acidity, and rather earthy overtones.

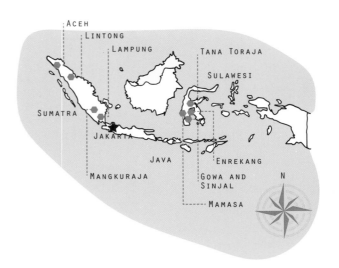

ACEH
LINTONG
LAMPUNG
TANA TORAJA
SULAWESI
SUMATRA
JAKARTA
JAVA
ENREKANG
MANGKURAJA
GOWA AND SINJAL
MAMASA
N

INDONESIA

Each island produces coffee with its own distinct characteristics.

Sumatra is Indonesia's largest island. Coffee is grown in the north (Aceh, Lintong) and the south (Lampung and Mangkuraja), at altitudes of between 2,600 and 5,000 ft. The coffee is dried using a process known as *giling basah* ("semiwashed"; see page 138), which lends the beans a characteristic bluish color.

Sulawesi is the island that produces the highest proportion of Arabica. The growing areas are located in the west and southwest of the island, at between 3,600 and 5,000 ft of altitude. The best known area is Tana Toraja, the highest part of the island, which provides the best conditions for coffee cultivation. The other areas are Mamasa, Enrekang, Gowa, and Sinjal. The most commonly grown Arabica variety is S795, a hybrid of Typica. Although the *giling basah* method is traditionally used, there are also some washed coffees to be found.

A large proportion of the coffee of Java is Robusta, grown in Indonesia's largest plantations at low altitude under government supervision (a legacy of the Dutch colonial era). Arabica is produced at altitudes of 4,600 to 5,900 ft. Javan coffee tends to be dried using the wet process.

KOPI LUWAK

These are coffee beans harvested from the droppings of the civet cat (called *luwak* in Indonesia). These mammals of Southeast Asia eat coffee cherries, digest the pulp, and expel the beans in their excrement. This discovery dates back to the eighteenth century, when the Indonesian plantations were owned by the Dutch, who banned local farmers from consuming the coffee beans, which were deemed a precious commodity and, at the time, intended for consumers in the West. So by harvesting coffee beans that had been pre-digested by civets, farmers were able to circumvent this ban. This type of coffee exhibits a particular flavor profile (it is said to be sweeter and richer) on account of fermentation that occurs during the digestion phase.

Kopi luwak is today part of global coffee folklore, and its success has prompted some unscrupulous producers to keep civets in cages and feed them coffee cherries (and not always the right kind) so as to generate more predigested coffee in order to meet market demand. These dubious practices, combined with very high prices, make kopi luwak a controversial product.

INDIA

Coffee is said to have been introduced to India in 1670 by Baba Budan, a pilgrim returning from Mecca. He is said to have carried seven coffee beans with him from Yemen, and planted them, with success, in the Chandragiri hills in the Karnataka region (in the west of the country). It was not until the nineteenth century, under the British, that the coffee trade took off. Arabica varieties predominated at that time, but leaf rust infestations prompted growers to switch to Robusta or hybrids (*arabica x liberica*), or even to give up coffee growing in favor of tea cultivation. In 1942, the Indian government decided to regulate coffee exports, and it was not until the 1990s that they were deregulated. Today India has around 250,000 producers working coffee plantations of less than 10 acres. Arabica varieties tend to be produced at altitudes of between 3,000 and 5,000 ft, under the shade of other exotic plants (pepper, cardamom, banana, vanilla, etc.).

THE FLAVORS OF AN INDIAN COFFEE:
MALABAR MOUSSONNÉ

COFFEE FACTS

▶ Annual production: 364,887 US tons (27.45% Arabica, 72.5% Robusta)

▶ World market share: 3.9%

▶ Producer's world ranking: 6th

▶ Principal varieties: Sarchimor, Kent, Catimor, S 795

▶ Harvest period(s): January–March

▶ Drying: monsooned, semiwashed, wet process, and dry process

▶ Characteristics: (see box: Monsooned Coffee)

MEGHALAYA
ARUNACHAL PRADESH
ASSAM
NEW DELHI
MANIPUR
TRIPURA
MIZORAM
ORISSA
ANDHRA PRADESH
KARNATAKA
KERALA
TAMIL NADU
N

COFFEE VARIETIES

SARCHIMOR

- **Origin:** hybrid (*villa sarchi x hibrido de Timor*)
- **Other producer countries:** Costa Rica, India
- **Resistance:** Its *Coffea canephora* genes make it highly resistant to leaf rust.
- **Yield:** decent (average of 2,200 lb/2.5 acres)
- **Recommended brewing method:** espresso
- **Cup:** not very high quality

HIBRIDO DE TIMOR

- **Origin:** Natural hybrid (*Coffea arabica x Coffea canephora*) discovered in Timor in the 1920s. This variety was used to produce various hybrids like Catimor, Sarchimor (*villa sarchi x hibrido de Timor*) in Brazil, and Ruiru 11 in Kenya.
- **Other producer country:** Indonesia
- **Plant:** this hybrid has 44 chromosomes, like all other Arabica varieties.
- **Resistance:** good
- **Yield:** decent (average of 2,200 lb/2.5 acres)
- **Recommended brewing method:** espresso
- **Cup:** not reputed for its flavor, owing to its Robusta genes

CATIMOR

- **Origin:** hybrid (*hibrido de Timor x caturra*) created in Portugal
- **Other producer countries:** Central America, South America
- **Plant:** normal size cherries
- **Resistance:** resistant, can cope with fairly low altitudes
- **Yield:** productive
- **Recommended preparation method:** espresso
- **Cup:** can be inferior (due to being partially derived from Timor, which is a hybrid of *Coffea arabica x Coffea canephora*).

MONSOONED COFFEE

India's most famous coffee is Monsoon Malabar, which has a very distinctive flavor profile as a result of its unique drying process. In the colonial era, green coffee beans being shipped from India to Europe were exposed to sea winds and moisture, causing them to swell and age prematurely and giving them a flavor like none other. To re-create this specific flavor today, green coffee beans are stored in open warehouses where they are exposed to humid monsoon air and absorb moisture. The swollen beans lose their natural acidity and turn pale. The coffee produces an earthy brew, without acidity but with a lot of body.

5

APPENDICES

USEFUL ADDRESSES & COFFEE EVENTS

Worldwide events

WCE (World Coffee Events)

World coffee championships (barista, brewer's cup, latte art, coffee in good spirits, cup tasters, roasting)

worldcoffeeevents.org

HOST Milan
Biennial

The SCAA Expo
Specialty Coffee Association of America, in the United States

MICE (Melbourne International Coffee Expo)
In Australia

National Aeropress championships
In more than forty countries

London Coffee Festival

New York Coffee Festival

Amsterdam Coffee Festival

CoLab
baristaguildofeurope.com/what-is-colab

Coffee shops around the world

PARIS

Coutume
47, rue de Babylone
75007 Paris
France

Dose
73, rue Mouffetard
75005 Paris
France

82, Place du Dr Félix
Lobligeois
75017 Paris
France

Honor
54, rue du Faubourg-Saint-
Honoré
75008 Paris
France

Loustic
40, rue Chapon
75003 Paris
France

LONDON

Association Coffee
10-12 Creechurch Ln
London EC3A 5AY
United Kingdom

Prufrock Coffee
23-25 Leather Ln
London EC1N 7TE
United Kingdom

Workshop Coffee
27 Clerkenwell Rd
London EC1M 5RN
United Kingdom

DUBLIN

3fe
32 Grand Canal St.
Lower, Dublin 2
Ireland

Meet Me in the Morning
50 Pleasants Street
Portobello, Dublin 8
Ireland

COPENHAGEN

The Coffee Collective
Odthåbsvej 34B
2000 Frederiksberg,
Denmark

OSLO

Tim Wendelboe
Grünersgate 1
0552 Oslo, Norvège

Supreme Roastwork
Thorvald Meyers Gate 18A
0474 Oslo
Norway

STOCKHOLM

Drop Coffee
Wollmar Yxkullsgatan 10
118 50 Stockholm
Sweden

FLORENCE

Ditta Artigianale
Via dei Neri, 32/R
50122 Florence
Italy

NEW YORK

Everyman Espresso
301 W Broadway
New York, NY 10013
United States

LAKEWOOD / DENVER

**Sweet Bloom Coffee
Roasters**
1619 Reed St.
Lakewood CO 80214
United States

LOS ANGELES

G&B Coffee
C-19, 317 S Broadway
Los Angeles CA 90013
United States

SEATTLE

Espresso Vivace
227 Yale Ave N
Seattle WA 98109
United States

MONTREAL

Cafe Myriade
1432 rue Mackay
Montréal QC H3G 2H7
Canada

TOKYO

Fuglen Tokyo
1-16-11 Tomigaya
Shibuya 151-0063
Japan

MELBOURNE

St Ali Coffee Roasters
12-18 Yarra Pl
South Melbourne VIC 3205
Australia

SÃO PAULO

Isso é Café
R. Carlos Comenale s/n
Bela Vista, São Paulo - SP
Brazil

COFFEE SHOP CAKES & COOKIES

Coffee shops often offer a selection of cakes and pastries to accompany one's coffee. Here are some of the well-known ones from French pastry chef Yohan Kim.

Carrot cake

Makes 8 to 10 servings

2½ OZ BUTTER, AT ROOM TEMPERATURE,
    PLUS MORE FOR THE PAN
7 OZ SUPERFINE SUGAR
3 EGGS
¼ TSP FINE SALT
10½ OZ ALL-PURPOSE FLOUR
1 OZ BAKING POWDER
¼ TSP GROUND CINNAMON
5 FL OZ PLAIN GREEK YOGURT
10½ OZ FINELY GRATED CARROTS
3½ OZ CHOPPED WALNUTS (OR HAZELNUTS,
    ALMONDS, ETC.)

1 Preheat the oven to 350°F. Grease a 9" x 5" baking pan with butter.

2 Beat together the butter and sugar until creamy and smooth.

3 Beat together the eggs and salt. Sift the flour, baking powder, and cinnamon into another bowl.

4 Incorporate the egg mixture, the dry ingredients, yogurt, grated carrots, and chopped nuts in turn into the butter-sugar mixture.

5 Pour the cake batter into the prepared pan and bake for 35 minutes.

6 Leave the carrot cake to cool in the pan, then turn it out and cut it into small squares.

> PERFECT WITH A CAPPUCCINO

Financiers

Makes 20 cakes

5½ OZ GROUND ALMONDS (ALMOND FLOUR)
3½ OZ SUPERFINE SUGAR
¾ OZ ALL-PURPOSE FLOUR
7 OZ EGG WHITES
5½ OZ BUTTER

1 Preheat the oven to 350°F.

2 Sift together the ground almonds, sugar, and flour.

3 Add the egg whites to the dry ingredients and mix.

4 Melt the butter in a microwave, add it to the mixture, and mix well.

5 Spoon the batter into a financier pan, dividing it among the individual molds, then bake for 9 to 10 minutes.

6 Leave the financiers to cool in the pan, then carefully release from their molds.

> PERFECT WITH AN ESPRESSO

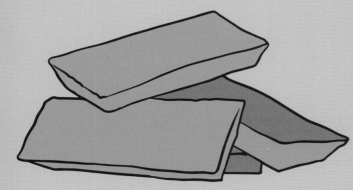

Chocolate cookies

Makes 20 cookies

4¼ OZ SUPERFINE SUGAR
5 EGGS
1¾ OZ ALL-PURPOSE FLOUR
1 OZ UNSWEETENED COCOA POWDER
1¾ OZ BUTTER, AT ROOM TEMPERATURE
3½ OZ DARK CHOCOLATE

1 Preheat the oven to 325°F. Line a baking sheet with parchment paper.

2 Beat the sugar and eggs together in a bowl until the mixture turns pale.

3 Sift the flour and cocoa powder together into a bowl, then incorporate the flour mixture into the sugar-egg mixture.

4 Using a spatula, work the butter to a creamy consistency. Break the chocolate into small chunks. Add the butter, then the chocolate to the mixture.

5 Place small spoonfuls of the dough on the prepared baking sheet, taking care to space them out, then bake for 15 to 20 minutes.

6 Leave the cookies to cool on the baking sheet, then carefully lift them off the parchment paper.

> PERFECT WITH AN ESPRESSO OR A FILTER COFFEE

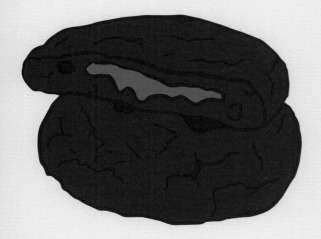

INDEX

THE AUTHORS

Chung-Leng Tran trained as a photographer before taking up a
new career as a barista. He was the French champion in the 2012
Brewers Cup. His coffee moments: a filter coffee (from Ethiopia or
Kenya) in the morning and an espresso after lunch.

Sébastien Racineux is a teacher of engineering and a barista
trainer. In 2011 he set up the Espressologie training organization.
He won the Coutume tournament in 2012, and was named French
vice-champion in the Brewers Cup in 2012 and 2014. His coffee
moment: an Ethiopian unwashed coffee midmorning.

In 2015, Sébastien and Chung-Leng, along with Stéphane Cataldi
and David Lahoz, opened their own roastery and coffee shop,
Hexagone Café, in Paris.

THE ILLUSTRATOR

Yannis Varoutsikos is an artistic director and illustrator. He has
illustrated several books for Marabout: *Le Vin c'est pas sorcier*
(2013), *Le Grand manuel du pâtissier* (2014), *Le Rugby c'est pas sorcier*
(2015), *Le Grand manuel du cuisinier* (2015). His coffee moments: a
Burundian coffee with his grandmother. Or a morning filter coffee
made in the Chemex. Thank you, Amandine!

ACKNOWLEDGMENTS

The authors would like to thank their families for their support.
They also wish to thank Stéphane Cataldi, roaster-traveler, for his
valuable advice; Yohan Kim for the cake and cookie recipes;
David Lahoz; Brian O'Keeffe; and Mikaël Portannier.

Black Dog & Leventhal Publishers
Hachette Book Group
1290 Avenue of the Americas
New York, NY 10104

www.hachettebookgroup.com
www.blackdogandleventhal.com

First English-language Edition: April 2018

Black Dog & Leventhal Publishers is an imprint of Hachette Books, a division of Hachette Book Group.
The Black Dog & Leventhal Publishers name and logo are trademarks of Hachette Book Group, Inc.

The publisher is not responsible for websites (or their content) that are not owned by the publisher.

The Hachette Speakers Bureau provides a wide range of authors for speaking events.
To find out more, go to www.HachetteSpeakersBureau.com or call (866) 376-6591.

Library of Congress Control Number: 2017949644

ISBNs: 978-0-316-43958-9 (hardcover); 978-0-316-43956-5 (ebook)

Printed in China
1010
10 9 8 7 6 5 4 3 2 1